Like Crazy

Also by Dan Mathews

Committed: A Rabble Rouser's Memoir

Like Crazy

Life with My Mother and Her Invisible Friends

Dan Mathews

ATRIA BOOKS

New York   London   Toronto   Sydney   New Delhi

An Imprint of Simon & Schuster, Inc.
1230 Avenue of the Americas
New York, NY 10020

First Atria Books hardcover edition May 2020

ATRIA BOOKS and colophon are trademarks of Simon & Schuster, Inc.

For information about special discounts for bulk purchases,
please contact Simon & Schuster Special Sales at 1-866-506-1949 or
business@simonandschuster.com.

The Simon & Schuster Speakers Bureau can bring authors to your live event.
For more information, or to book an event, contact the Simon &
Schuster Speakers Bureau at 1-866-248-3049 or visit our
website at www.simonspeakers.com.

Interior design by Alexis Minieri

Manufactured in the United States of America

1   3   5   7   9   10   8   6   4   2

Library of Congress Cataloging-in-Publication Data has been applied for.

ISBN 978-1-5011-9998-1
ISBN 978-1-9821-0001-8 (ebook)

To Eleanor, Mary Ellen, Ellen Marston, Perry Lawrence,
and any other handle Mom used in her eighty-two years

"Have I not told you that what you mistake for madness is but overacuteness of the senses?"

—EDGAR ALLAN POE

WINTER 2008

Chapter 1

OVERWHELMED
IN OLDE TOWNE

"I want my children to have all the things I couldn't afford.
Then I want to move in with them."
—Phyllis Diller

Dusk fell quickly as I braced for my mother's chaotic December arrival in Virginia.

Dead leaves and lively carolers swirled around Olde Towne Portsmouth's warped cobblestone streets. Tinsel-lined, fogged-up bar windows advertised mulled wine. The brick square in front of the 1846 courthouse was festooned with luminous Christmas clowns. Their creaky mechanical arms mystified red-cheeked children.

The neon glow of the deco movie palace on High Street beckoned clutches of merry-makers wrapped in scarves. Where High Street runs into the river, crowds formed a single-file line for

Portsmouth's paddlewheel ferry to Norfolk, a service that has chugged along since 1636. Passengers hurried aboard to cross the harbor before seven. That's when the holiday lights atop Norfolk's mini-skyscrapers were switched on, signaling the start of the Grand Illumination Parade. Marching bands played brassy holiday tunes, as plump majorettes in white knee-high boots twirled batons and strutted to the beat. Their panting breath sent bursts of mist into the first chilly air of the season.

Usually I am on the curb cheering them on. That year I was at home, overwhelmed in Olde Towne, cheering on a wiry, white-haired, self-proclaimed Jesus freak. His name was Steve Self and his business card read Self Service. I hired him to help fix up the rickety old house I had just bought for my rickety old mother and me. Mr. Self wore faded blue jeans and a utility belt. He wielded power tools for the heavy jobs, while I handled decorations. Such as a flag featuring a gingerbread man with a chunk missing from his leg and the message "Bite Me," which I hoisted over the porch.

For motivation, I blasted my usual Christmas playlist: a disco version of "Silver Bells," Charo's "Mamacita Dónde Está Santa Claus?" and a blues ballad called "Daddy's Drinkin' Up Our Christmas"—a tune that hit too close to home for my evangelical handyman. Mr. Self looked up from the pink shag carpet he was laying in the downstairs bedroom intended for Mumsie and let out a groan. Having given up liquor after some hard-partying years, he became born again as a means of leaving the past behind and starting anew. Whatever it takes.

In a clumsy attempt to correct the musical faux pas, I skipped ahead to the next track. It was an obscure country rant called "Here Comes Fatty with His Sack of Shit."

"That's a little better." Mr. Self laughed in his raspy southern drawl. "But don't you have any spirituals?"

"Sure do!" Lawrence Welk's accordion interpretation of "Do You Hear What I Hear?" was in there somewhere.

Mr. Self was a godsend. He was the contractor hired by the realtor to replace shattered windows and broken pipes when I made the rash decision to buy the dilapidated Victorian. I asked him to stay on to sand the splintered hardwood floors, install a senior-friendly sit-down shower for Mommie Dearest, and jack up my bathroom sink upstairs so I wouldn't throw out my back when I bent my six-foot-five frame in to shave.

Mr. Self helped me paint each room a different color from the Crayola Crayons Paint Collection: Tickle Me Pink, Shamrock, Neon Carrot, Radical Red, Banana Mania, and B'dazzled Blue. My house looks like a rainbow burst through a window and hemorrhaged all over the place. Once the chemical fumes from the paint had faded, Mr. Self drilled holes in the walls and installed thrift shop sconces, on which I placed candles, vintage photos of oddball strangers, and souvenir shot glasses.

Out of respect for his religious beliefs, I hid my framed *Exorcist* poster of a possessed Linda Blair in the closet until he was finished. I could not resist, however, screwing on my light-socket plate of a cartoon hunk, his blue bathrobe flung open so that the switch dangles between his legs. As electrical accessories go, it's a turn-on. My pious carpenter chuckled and shook his head when he saw it. Mr. Self was devout but not disparaging. When he invoked a Bible passage, it sounded more like he was trying to recall his Social Security number than espouse morals. As an atheist in southern Virginia, I've learned to sidestep religion and politics and find common ground with any interesting individual I encounter. While I do not believe in gods above and devils below, I do honor the instinct inside that tells you the right thing to do. That's why I decided to buy a house and move in my ill, unhinged mother.

Her name, which she changed many times over the decades, was now Perry. I addressed her as Mom—or in heated conversations "*Mother!*" My friends called her Perry so I often did, too. Sometimes she referred to herself as Paris, pronounced in the French way: Paree! Whatever the name, my friends were uniformly shocked when I announced that I would be taking her in. They listed the many ways my life would be derailed:

"You're not much of a family man." "You love living alone." "You barely have the patience to stay overnight with your mother once a year; how would you tolerate being around her all the time?"

I travel a lot with work, so hopefully I won't feel too trapped.

"You work for PETA and pinch your nose at the stench of meat."

Perry hasn't eaten meat since the eighties.

"What about having boyfriends over and impromptu late-night parties."

She would love that. She always wanted to be a fag hag but never had the social skills. Plus she's nearly deaf. I could play music at any hour.

"You've never owned a house, only rented bachelor pads—how will you maintain a home and a full-time job while looking after a sick old woman?"

Ouch. This one was tough to answer. I was such a gadabout that I had deemed myself unqualified to care for a low-maintenance plant, much less a high-maintenance parent. Was I as nuts as my mom?

Taking in Perry was not a decision to make lightly. Long troubled by the way Americans discard seniors like cigarette butts, I read up on how other countries dealt with the aged in hopes of inspiration. In Tamil Nadu, elders are gently bathed in fragrant yet lethal oils that cause kidney failure; alas, Mom was too hobbled to climb into a tub. In ancient Japan, old people were brought high into the hills and abandoned; Virginia has so many damned hiking trails that she would be found before I made it to the after-party. Inuits set their withering parents adrift on ice floes, another tradition ruined by global warming.

Enough with the fantasies. There was no shirking this responsibility. I felt duty-bound to look after my mother. I couldn't stick her in some nearby apartment where I'd count the minutes during visits, nor in assisted living, where dead neighbors are whisked out the back door each week like expired brisket. We had to be under the same roof, enjoying life in our own house. Neither of us had ever owned one.

Could I become responsible enough to be the head of a household, learn what a mortgage was, and do home repairs? Mom and I were hopeless in a hardware store. To us a screwdriver wasn't a tool but a cocktail. My only repair kit was a small blue plastic foldout case meant for single ladies called "Do It Herself," with wrenches that looked like they belonged in Barbie's Dream House. To make this mission a success, I would need guidance from anyone who offered it, starting with my saintly handyman.

As he showed me the difference between a Phillips and a flathead (I generally used a butter knife), Mr. Self said, "It's a blessing you're taking in your ailing mama, but it sure would be easier on you if you were married."

I arched an eyebrow. "I'm not the marrying kind. Plus my kind isn't allowed to marry. At least not yet in Virginia."

"Well," he said, looking away sheepishly, "God bless you anyways."

"I appreciate that. And I am blessed with good friends. One of them is flying in with her from Los Angeles tomorrow."

Chapter 2

HOME STRETCH

"Thank God I have this oxygen mask—people fart nonstop on airplanes." So declared my seventy-eight-year-old mother as she boarded the packed flight at Los Angeles International Airport, or LAX.

Hard of hearing, she hollered without realizing it. Thus the remark reverberated through the United Airlines cabin like an overhead announcement. According to my tall ex-boyfriend Diego, who was kind enough to accompany her on the red-eye, Mom's statement turned heads as she limped up the aisle wheeling an air tank and clutching a floral medicine tote. Towering behind the hunched white-haired granny, Diego struggled with two quivering cat carriers.

Mom was so ill the week before she flew to Virginia that she went from the hospital directly to the airport. She had no luggage except a carry-on and Daisy and Sydney, her feisty felines, whom Diego had scooped up. Mom had COPD: chronic obstructive pulmonary disease, which makes breathing difficult.

"You must delay the trip until you've recovered from this latest bout," Mom's doctor ordered at her bedside, flanked by my two vexed brothers, Mike and Pat. Ignoring the advice, she made her getaway with my ex as her henchman. Impulsive episodes like this intrigued me as a kid, but caused me to flee across multiple time zones after high school. It had been more than twenty years since I felt that tinge of anxiety about Mom's manic behavior. Now, as her (gulp) guardian, I would be dealing with it on a daily basis.

Once Perry, Diego, and the two shrieking cats reached their row near the back of the plane, Mom texted me: "I will not croak in L.A." Long unable to hear over a phone, she quickly took to texting, with the zeal of a teen. With arthritic fingers whose pink nails needed a touch-up, Mom typed, "I'm making this move now even if I drop dead at the arrivals gate in Norfolk."

I read her message in my half-finished house sipping a full glass of wine. Her dramatic departure from LAX brought me back to a scene from my childhood that unfolded at the very same airport. The incident marked the first time I truly sensed something was amiss with Mother.

I was nine at the time. My brothers and I were returning from a two-week summer vacation in Florida, where we visited our father, Ray, and new stepmother, Joan. They rented an RV and took us on an exotic road trip. We marveled at the dancing mermaids at Weeki Wachee Springs, sped around the Everglades on an airboat, and explored the recently opened Disney World. We were unable to call home and check in with Mom as our phone service had been cut off (again). Instead, we scribbled postcards to her every few days and looked forward to recounting our adventures as soon as we returned.

Mom greeted us at our gate looking glamorous but fragile. She had casually styled dark blonde hair, frosty pink lips, and baby blue eyes that were dripping tears and traces of mascara. We merely thought she was overjoyed to see us. But when we hugged, she convulsed in sobs. What awful thing had happened while we were away? Finally, she sighed relief and regarded us with weighty seriousness.

"Don't worry, boys—your father will never kidnap you again."

My brothers and I exchanged the usual look of exasperation at one of Mom's meltdowns. But the magnitude felt greater this time. It was beyond the occasional divorcée diva fit.

"We weren't kidnapped," I said, forcing a smile. "We were on a road trip; didn't you get the postcards?"

"Yes, but they didn't fool me. I heard what happened and I've been to see a lawyer."

"Heard what, from who?" asked my older brother Mike, trying to reason with her. "We don't have the money for a phone but you've seen a lawyer about a kidnapping that didn't happen?"

"We went to Cape Canaveral!" added my younger brother Pat.

"I don't want to talk about it," she whimpered. "I'm just glad to have you kids back safe."

Disheartened, we went from skipping off the plane to trudging through the terminal. Previously, whenever Mom seemed paranoid or delusional, I had written it off to the circumstances: an irksome employer, unfair landlord, untrustworthy neighbor, or a spat with ever-patient Dad. He moved clear across the country after their eleven-year marriage imploded. He rarely spoke to her or about her, not even disparagingly. It was all a big mystery. That day, as we made our way through the crowded airport, I detected in Mom a puzzling trait. An emotion beyond her control put her in an alternate reality. Arguing over the occasional delusions only made matters worse.

I changed the subject to our favorite show. "I hope the season premiere of *Carol Burnett* has a 'Mama's Family' skit."

"That would be wonderful." Mom sniffled, wiping her eyes as we exited the terminal.

"*Will you cheer up, Mama?!*" I yelped in a prepubescent drawl, imitating Eunice, the Carol Burnett character who gets flustered with her own neurotic "Mama." I often mimicked Eunice's wisecracks as a roundabout way of acknowledging our own crises. "*Mama, you're gettin' furrows in your forehead from all that frownin'!*"

Mom chuckled and the dark spell was broken. Mike zigzagged the luggage cart with Pat riding on top, our beat-up Galaxie 500 miraculously started on the fourth try, and everything was back to normal for a while. Such was our life in the seventies.

Now, more than three decades later, Mom was back at LAX. Not as glamorous, but just as much a drama queen. Diego told me that once she was in her seat, Perry removed her oxygen mask and flagged a flight attendant.

"Excuse me, how long into the flight will dinner be served?"

"I'm sorry, ma'am, there's food service only in first class."

"I see," Mom replied politely. "That's why I'm a communist." Diego burst into laughter, thinking she was joking. Still giggling, he crammed the cat carriers under the seats in front of them. The sedative prescribed by the vet had finally sent the adopted kitties to dreamland. Mom always had an affinity for strays. Not just cats, but any wayward creature. Including several loveable loners I befriended over the years—like Diego.

Mom often became a surrogate mother to misfit friends of mine, especially to those rejected by their own parents. When my childhood best friend Michael contracted AIDS, he reluctantly came out to his parents, only for his mother to say, "I'd rather you told me you were a serial killer." Mom took charge by moving in with Michael to nurse and entertain him as he wasted away. At that point, I lived across the country, but she dutifully called and put Michael on the phone so we could reminisce, even as he started slipping into a coma and could only respond with sighs.

If someone was down, Perry came 'round. Because she had so often assumed the role of an irreverent Florence Nightingale, even when her own health failed, I quickly ran out of excuses as to why I couldn't look after her.

As Perry's reckless move to Virginia grew near, Diego, her latest protégé, was eager to help. He offered to escort her on the plane, freeing up more time for Mr. Self and me to work on the house. To be candid, Diego was a very experienced escort—though his clients were not usually little old ladies on airplanes, but closeted businessmen in hotel rooms.

Diego and I first met in Las Vegas. I had flown in to lead a PETA protest at a fashion convention, while he was there to "entertain" male conventioneers for whom the slogan "what happens in Vegas, stays in Vegas" was especially apt. After work, we each ended up at a gay club. As the tallest guys there, we naturally caught one another's eye. Diego was handsome, soft-spoken, introspective, and intriguing. He charmed me by reciting a dark poem about Sin City, though I could barely hear it above the din of the dance floor. We ditched the loud bar for a quiet walk and a passionate night in a dumpy room at the Imperial Palace. He didn't tell me about his livelihood until the next morning.

"I'd like to see you again," he stammered nervously. "But I want to tell you how I support myself so there are no surprises later."

"Are you a hit man?" I half-joked. "If so, do you do pro bono work and take suggestions?"

"No, fool. I'm an escort. Just until I get myself through nursing school. I'm totally safe, but some guys can't handle it."

Diego had already told me that he grew up in a large religious family, so it was a bit of a shocker. Though statuesque, his casual style did not suggest "Vegas gigolo." I never imagined being in this situation and didn't know how to feel. I really liked Diego (an alias) and wanted to see him again, so I just shrugged it off. Like most of us, I occasionally succumbed to foolish jealousy. Maybe dating a hustler would help me overcome that awful trait.

I introduced Diego to my mother on our first rendezvous in California. He was captivated by her brash humor and the fact that she didn't judge anyone unless they wore a fanny pack. Given his conservative upbringing, Diego was astounded that Perry so easily accepted him, not only for being gay but also as her son's boyfriend. They bonded over her collection of Mexican history books and Dame Edna videos and kept in touch, often emailing each other articles from *The Onion*.

When I confided in Mom about Diego's saucy source of income, her eyes grew wide. She shushed me. After thinking for a moment, she imparted her brand of motherly advice. "*Never* refer to Diego as a hustler. Just say that he's in real estate—and manages a very large rental property."

After Mom absconded with Diego, my brothers sorted her stuff. They shipped boxes of collectibles to us in Portsmouth. *Simpsons* and *Star Wars* Pez dispensers, programs from her favorite *Nutcracker* performances, campaign buttons for candidates she volunteered for since JFK. Xeroxed letters she wrote to comics who quipped a line she found worth repeating. A few sent grateful personal replies, which she saved in her files.

Lining Mom's kitchen shelves were dozens of ceramic, glass, and steel cream pitchers she had nonchalantly emptied and slipped into her purse at diners over the decades. This compulsion earned her the nickname "Cream Pitcher Perry." Mom was not a kleptomaniac, but for some reason she couldn't resist pilfering the little decanters.

Harder to pack were the books.

Mom had a few hundred hardbacks. We lugged them from apartment to apartment when we were kids. Her tattered library included espionage memoirs (she always wanted to be a spy), Will and Ariel Durant's *Story of Civilization* series, and every book by political satirist Art Buchwald, who, like Mom, grew up in foster homes and orphanages during the Great Depression. Home was always a fleeting thing for my mother. This made her final relocation to Virginia most meaningful.

Mom was born with neither a name nor an address on her birth certificate—a predicament that would forever jinx her.

Without a foster parent, a spouse, a friend, or one of her kids to help her along, her life was one big housing crisis. It wasn't merely a financial struggle. She often found work as a bookkeeper through temp agencies. Rather, she lacked the desire and ability to remain in one place for more than a few years. We assumed this was a pattern set in place by her rootless childhood.

A few years after my brothers and I had left California for college, Mom sent us each a breezy postcard: "I've moved into the Salvation Army in downtown LA—there are so many wonderful museums I can walk to!"

After this short stint on Skid Row—which upset Mike, Pat, and me much more than it did Mom—we three boys took turns helping her get apartments. Mostly in Southern California, where Mike and Pat (and Dad and Joan) had resettled. Over time, my brothers' lives grew increasingly complicated. They sprouted families of their own, with wives, ex-wives, in-laws, ex-in-laws, and lots of kids. I, being a happy-go-lucky homosexual, had carefully avoided all of that. This meant, of course, that the deviant son was stuck with the crazy mother. Like Norman Bates in *Psycho*.

Mom landed in Norfolk around the four hundredth anniversary of the arrival of British colonists. The patriotic fervor was inescapable. Against all odds, the settlers had turned Virginia tribal grounds into tobacco plantations, replaced the natives with slaves, and produced a crop that would provide the world with centuries of cancer. The wily entrepreneurs were saluted on inspirational billboards with the slogan "Determination: Pass It On." Mom noticed one as we drove out of the airport.

"*Bastards,*" she hissed. She looked like ghostly Grandmama from *The Addams Family* after the overnight flight. She was also giddy about seeing her new home.

A tree obscures the street sign on our easily overlooked lane, often causing first-time visitors to miss the turn and get lost. Friends have said the Gothic block is not in Portsmouth but the *Twilight Zone*. It consists largely of detached eighteenth- and nineteenth-century pastel houses, with vine-laden terraces overlooking redbrick sidewalks.

Our two-story wooden Victorian is sky blue, with a simple façade that belies the oddly shaped rooms, alcoves, hidden staircase, and straggly backyard. Because of the color and the ease with which you can lose yourself in the mazelike property, I sometimes call it my "Wild Blue Yonder."

To keep it safe from hurricane surges, the house was erected half a story up from the street. This makes it appear grander than it is. A curved set of steps leads from the street to a wide, white-columned porch and a heavy oak door with beveled glass. The front of the house looks radiant in the morning sun—perfect timing for Mom's arrival.

We came to a stop on the crunchy gravel lane. Diego and I helped Mom climb out of my avocado Suzuki Sidekick. She looked at the rustic fixer-upper with wide-eyed wonder, as if it were the Hearst Castle.

"*Wow!*"

Then she looked at the six stairs as if they were the Rockies.

"*Fuck!*"

I helped her ease slowly up the stairs as Diego unloaded the cats. Trembling but overjoyed, she paused on each step and looked around to take in her new surroundings. Across from our place is a tidy park with a winding path leading to tombstones of soldiers from the American Revolution and the War of 1812.

The only sounds were distant horns in the harbor, faint train whistles, and birds chirping in the pines. On this morning, we also heard the clink of steel scissors, which the old man next door used to clip his wall of ivy.

I chose the house not just for the price and privacy. It was the only one with a first-floor bedroom for stair-wary Perry. Plus, it's only a few streets from the library, the coffee shop, the old movie theater, the ferry, and several bars and restaurants. Since Mom no longer drove, she could easily totter to these destinations with her cane, rather than be stranded in the suburbs as she had been in California.

When she at last reached the porch, she held on to a column and announced to the meowing cats, "We are finally home—and we're never moving again!"

The adventure was under way. I was so proud that I stopped worrying for a moment that the heat had just been cut off. Despite the December chill, in my rush to get the house ready and caught up at work, I had forgotten to have the service continued.

Mom slept for three days under four blankets. Daisy sat sentry on her bed and Sydney hid underneath. She awoke with a sluggish smile only when Diego and I brought her soup or propped a mirror under her nose to see if it fogged. Mom's frustrated doctor out west called and said that if she rested after the "foolhardy trip" and kept taking the antibiotics she would soon rebound.

While Perry slumbered like a septuagenarian Sleeping Beauty, Diego and I decorated her room. We fastened an ornate wooden yard-sale headboard to her bed. Above it, we hung her poster of Giulietta Masina, the quirky star of Fellini classics. Masina won Oscars for her intense portrayals of naïve characters dealing with cruel circumstances, predicaments my mother identified with.

We displayed Perry's diploma from Orange Coast College on her dresser. It took her eleven years of evening courses to earn, while raising three kids and working multiple jobs. Mom never attended high school. Instead, she opted to work in order to flee the last of her foster homes—the one in which she was repeatedly molested. At her triumphant college graduation, in an emerald cap and gown, Mom wept even more uncontrollably than she did when John Belushi OD'd.

With the room set up, I took Diego out for a bittersweet farewell dinner. My daunting new responsibilities as a homeowner and a caregiver—in addition to my full-time job as an animal rights activist—meant I was no longer free to enjoy weekend flings with Diego out west. He was too entrenched in school to visit Virginia. We had dated off and on for six years, and now we would just be friends.

Roused from her bed on Diego's last day, Mom shuffled in her nightgown through the kitchen to our cozy den. Logs blazed in the fireplace. A pair of wooden thrones upholstered in red velvet flanked the floor-to-ceiling front windows. A church must have dropped them off at Goodwill minutes before I'd arrived and bought them. Between the thrones, a tall Douglas fir flashed silver snowflake lights. The makeshift angel we strapped on top was Mom's favorite doll: the Sweet Transvestite action figure from *Rocky Horror.*

"Oh, Danny Lee!" Mom exclaimed. She used my middle name only in her most emotional moments.

Diego led her to one of the regal red chairs. She sat with dangling feet and moist eyes staring at the fire. An expression of pure joy washed over her face. For her final act, Mom had successfully fled suburban isolation for a vibrant life in a quirky, walkable harbor town. And Christmas was right around the corner!

Chapter 3

BETTER WATCH OUT

Within a week, Mom felt rejuvenated enough to break free from the oxygen tank and venture out of the house. On sunny days when I was at work, she bundled up in her Michelin Man coat, grabbed her cane, and explored Olde Towne. Since some sections of the brick sidewalk erupt with thick roots, Mom hobbled along in the more evenly paved gutter.

Heading from our house to the river, she trudged down Dinwiddie Street, where Benedict Arnold marched with British troops. There is a Revolutionary War marker about him near the embankment. It's a popular pee spot for dogs trotting along with their companions in scrubs from the nearby Naval Hospital. Mom often perched on a bench there with a book, though she fussed with the dogs more than she read. One of those dogs belonged to a sociable young navy doctor and nurse couple. Mike and Abby soon came over with a bottle of wine and became friends.

At lunchtime, Mom often traipsed to High Street for fries at Griff's Irish Pub. There she met a regular named Carl, a husky blond immigrant with a Galway brogue. As Mom's hazy lineage traces to the Emerald Isle, all things Irish fascinated her. Between Carl's strong accent and Perry's weak hearing, I don't know how they communicated. He stopped by the house between carpentry jobs to chat and bring her newspapers sent by his family in the home country.

One Saturday morning, Mom accompanied me up Middle Street to A Touch of Style, Olde Towne's busiest barbershop. My hair was long and I wanted to keep it that way for winter, but it was wavy and unruly. I had the dumb idea to get it straightened with a chemical relaxer, which the feisty bald stylist refused to do, saying my hair would fall out.

"You want your head to look like mine?" he joked.

"I was just curious to see if I could keep my hair long without it being so damned bushy," I naïvely explained. That produced a belly laugh from the stylists and customers alike in the bustling salon. Mom and I were the only white clientele.

"You're most welcome here," said the barber, "but we specialize in afros and a relaxer would fry you. We can't do that. Though we sure can tease ya!"

Deaf Perry sat with a grin, pretending to understand why everyone was chortling. Embarrassed but undeterred, I settled for a precision cut, some well-deserved teasing, and an orange tub of Murray's Superior Hair Pomade.

Portsmouth is 52 percent black. Racism festers everywhere, but it feels less toxic here than in Washington, DC, where I lived before PETA relocated. Transplants from Chicago and Nashville have made similar comparisons. This may be because Portsmouth is a navy town; the military was integrated after World War II. The 1948 order by President Eisenhower gave our city a generational head start on government-sanctioned equality, which did not trickle into other towns until after the Civil Rights Act of 1964. It shows in the blasé attitude toward two-toned couples at the grocery store and mixed cliques at bars and parties.

I witnessed a similar social phenomenon after President Obama repealed "Don't Ask, Don't Tell," allowing gays to serve openly in the military. Ironically, the change I noticed most wasn't in the behavior of the gay sailors I knew, but in the attitudes of straight enlisted men, especially in dive bars near the shipyard. Many who had previously been aloof, uneasy, or even hostile to my gay friends and me suddenly embraced us as "bros" and bought us shots.

The week before Christmas, Mom felt strong enough to explore beyond our fair city. I picked her up after work for dinner at a Mexican joint to plan a Saturday trip to Richmond. In chipper spirits, we made our way back to my Sidekick in the chilly night, arm in arm. Mom had decided to stop using her cane when she was with me in public, lamenting, "That thing makes me look so damn feeble." The restaurant's empty parking lot was so dark you could barely make out the speed bumps.

I guided her to the car, keeping watch for any debris on which she might trip. I opened the passenger door, and as she started to get in, I walked around to the driver's side. The next sound should have been her door closing. Instead, there was a crunching sound, like eggshells shattering. When I looked over, Mom was on the ground.

Her skull had smashed into the pavement.

She had fallen backward out of the car while climbing in, and now there was a petrifying silence. Within seconds, I was at her side on the blacktop, but during those terrifying seconds, because of her stillness, I actually thought she might be dead—just a few weeks after moving in with me. I breathed a sigh of relief when I saw her eyes open and her chest heaving.

"Can you move?"

"Yes, I think so, but let me just lay here a second."

Trying to control my own panicked breath, I grabbed a towel from the hatchback. When I lifted her head to slide it underneath, I saw a trace of blood.

"Let's call an ambulance."

"No," she said calmly. "It'll be quicker and easier to drive to the ER; I'm sure I can get up."

My friend Jeff worked at Harbor View Hospital just two miles away. I called his cell and, luckily, he was an admitting physician that night. Jeff's last name is Holliday, so of course we all call him Doc Holliday. He has striking good looks and a warm bedside manner. With curly black hair and a confident grin, he looks like a well-built New York Jew, though he's really a Gentile from Louisiana.

I had no idea that Jeff was a doctor when I first met him at the YMCA. I thought he might well be a backup dancer for Beyoncé. At the gym, Doc ditches his white lab coat for the latest neon, spandex banana hammock exercise getups from the International Male catalog. His heart patients would have had coronaries if they saw him at the Y.

"I've been looking forward to meeting you, Perry!" Doc said as he helped her into a wheelchair. "But not like this. We're gonna have to get you a football helmet."

"I hate football, I'd never wear it," she replied with a flirty smile, her white hair streaked with blood. I tensely pushed the wheelchair as Doc Holliday led us to a private room.

"Why did you fall—did you have a blackout?"

"No. Just clumsy I guess."

Doc swiveled her around so he could inspect her wound under the bright examination light. On the back of Mom's pale skull was an intricate road map of veins leading to a bloody swollen splotch in the center. It looked as if the creature from *Alien* was trying to escape. Normally, it's easy for me to be as lighthearted as they were, but in this instance I was too upset to join in the banter. I was furious with myself for failing to make sure Mom was in the car with the door shut before moving around to the driver's side. Maybe my friends were right. Was I conscientious enough to look after a frail senior?

Doc shined a penlight in Mom's eyes. He asked her to turn her head in each direction.

"Believe it or not, as bad as this looks, I don't even think it's a concussion. We'll have to get X-rays to be sure, but you don't need to be admitted. It'll just be a really big bruise."

"Well, then I'll just have to wear a hat on our trip to Richmond!"

"What you really need is a medical alert necklace," Doc said. "What if you fall when nobody is around?"

"I hate the bitch in those commercials."

"There are lots of different brands. You don't have to buy that one."

"Thank you. I may be a pathetic old lady, but I refuse to look like one."

Late Saturday morning, I made sure Perry was in the Sidekick with the door closed before getting in myself. She wore a white synthetic shearling cap with matching scarf to ward off the chill—and to conceal the eggplant emanating from her cranium. The ninety-minute drive to Richmond went by in no time as we listened to big-band Christmas tunes on the 1940s station.

After cruising around the eerie mansions on Church Hill, we made our way to Grace Street to pay our respects to Elizabeth Van Lew, our favorite Civil War hero. She turned her wealthy family's hilltop estate into a spy ring to defeat the Confederacy in its own capital. Van Lew got her black maid Mary a job in the Confederate White House in order to smuggle out battle plans to Union generals. Nobody suspected the house cleaner or the spinster.

However, after the war, when General Grant declared that her elaborate espionage was key to the Union victory, Van Lew was shunned by Richmond society. Children crossed the street when she walked by and called her a witch. One of her last public appearances was protesting the 1890 unveiling of the monument to Robert E. Lee, who, she pointed out, opposed the monument himself before his death. Elizabeth died a pauper, and city officials tore down her grand home overlooking the James River. All that remains is a historical marker. If you had driven by that marker when Mom and I were paying our respects, you might have thought we were laying daisies where a relative was shot.

Still dabbing our eyes on the drive down the hill, we stopped for carrot soup and hummus at Café Gutenberg. The busy hangout had elegant racks of newspapers from around the world for customers to peruse, as well as hometown papers. Mom laid out the plethora of pills she took each day, while I flipped through the local weekly. Southern Culture on the Skids, a band I had long wanted to see, was playing that night. I showed Mom the listing, which called them "swamp rock's bards of downward mobility" alongside a rave review of their album, *Liquored Up and Lacquered Down*.

"We were led here!" Mom yelped, always the fatalist. "Let's spend the night and see them! It will be so loud even I can hear. The cats are fed and will be fine till tomorrow."

I was elated. Mom, despite her age and feebleness, remained as spontaneous as ever. This was why she rushed across the country in an oxygen mask. To reinvigorate whatever was left of her life with the only person who would actually enjoy indulging her whims. We paid up and drove around to find a place to crash.

Richmond's Linden Row Inn is a corner strip of Greek Revival town houses surrounding a landscaped courtyard. Edgar Allan Poe played there as a child. The enchanted garden Poe wrote about in *To Helen* was inspired by this courtyard, where he found solitude after his mother's death. Gothic lore, plus Christmas décor? We checked in immediately.

"It's lovely but it's *freezing*," Mom said as we entered the high-ceilinged room we were to share on the third floor. She cranked up the heat and flopped down on the bed to rest an hour before the concert.

At ten o'clock, we arrived at the dank club just as the opening band finished. The tattooed behemoth at the ticket window was so bemused to see an old lady that he refused to charge her—or me—admission. I made a mental note to bring Perry to clubs more often.

We found seats along the wall of the jammed venue. I fetched us each a bourbon and ginger before the band—a wiry hillbilly guitarist, a perky singer in a red bouffant, a rowdy drummer in overalls, and an obese bassist in a wifebeater—took the stage. It was a mesmerizing show, especially when they played their rockabilly hit, "Daddy Was a Preacher But Momma Was a Go-Go Girl."

"I can hear, I can hear!" Mom yelled over the commotion, as if we were at a revival. We left just before the end in order to beat the crowd. Mom had again refused to bring her cane. We exited through the side door and meandered carefully through a dark alley to the car.

The Linden Row was silent when we returned just after midnight. Mom was winded but in great spirits. As we awaited the sluggish, antiquated elevator, we looked out onto the spooky courtyard. When the door lurched open, Mom shambled toward it ahead of me. Like a toddler, she dragged her feet across the elevator's uneven gap.

Perry went down like a chain-sawed sequoia.

Unable to lift her arms to break the fall, her face clanked full-force into the steel handrail at the back of the elevator. Then it bounced up before she crumbled facedown onto the floor. A pool of blood formed. Just as when she fell from the car a few nights before, there was no scream. Just a spine-chilling stillness.

"Mom!"

The creaky door closed on her motionless legs, then sprung back open as I leapt in and knelt beside her. Because she was facedown, I couldn't see whether her eyes were open, if she was breathing, or if she had a pulse. I felt as if my own heart might stop.

Finally, after several seconds, there was a slurred response.

"This time, I'm dead," she mumbled, lips in the gritty flat carpet. "Just leave me here."

I called 911 and extended my foot to jam the elevator door open, to keep it from ramming Mom's legs.

"They'll be right here," I said, trying to keep calm. "Just hold on."

As the agonizing minutes passed until help arrived, I glanced from the elevator back into the garden where Poe mourned his mother. Might I soon be using the grounds for the same purpose?

———

When a beat-up senior rolls into a hospital, it's routine to treat the patient as a possible victim of elder abuse. These cases spike during the holidays. Tense family members endure long days of small talk with a cranky cousin, an alcoholic uncle, or a disapproving grandmother whom they'd like to clobber on the head—and sometimes do.

The check-in nurse gave me a grim gaze when I strode into the tinsel-lined ER. It was the second time that week I had to roll Bloody Perry into a trauma unit. Her face looked like a Meat Lover's Pizza. As we would soon learn, Mom's headfirst plummet into the elevator railing resulted in several small fractures around her chin, cheekbones, and eye sockets. Her puffy black eyes and bloody gashes were disturbing to others, but in the ambulance, Mom's chief concern was making me fumble through her purse to find her camera. With a grotesque grin, she said, "I'll never look like this again."

Ensconced behind a hospital curtain, I stopped shuddering enough to open the lens cap. Mom posed on the gurney like a freshly battered belle as I nervously flashed snapshots to memorialize the moment. Mid-click, the curtain was whisked open. A shocked doctor and nurse glowered at me. The party was over.

"What are you doing?" the doctor asked.

"She wanted a few photos for posterity," I replied defensively.

Mom couldn't hear the exchange clearly; she just squinted up at us through tiny slits in the purple golf balls that were her eyes.

"Wait outside," said the nurse. "We'll need to speak with her alone."

"But she's practically deaf. I'm her son and translator."

The nurse said nothing. She simply held the curtain back

with a stern gesture for me to wait in the nearby reception area. I waved goodbye to Mom. She replied by wiggling the hand that was not being attached to tubes.

Because the doctor had to bellow like Pavarotti for Perry to understand his questions, the whole ER heard him repeatedly ask how she fell.

"*Was someone else involved in the accident?*"

Mom finally realized what he meant and began cackling.

"No! Stop it!" she said, her speech slurred like the *Elephant Man*. "It hurts like hell to laugh, just give me drugs!" After later exchanges carried out on a notepad—and after the doctor embroidered her face with stitches—Mom was released to my questionable care just before dawn.

Before Perry's horrific tumbles, we had been planning a Christmas Eve movie party so that I could introduce her to friends and coworkers. I figured she would have bounced back from the heart and lung crisis by then. Little did I know her face would look like she had just lost a mixed martial arts bout. Even the cats did a double take when Mom greeted them upon our return. After the traumatic ordeal, I couldn't imagine either of us carrying on with the party. Though I hated to cancel this one.

Every Christmas Eve, I show the 1974 Margot Kidder cult film *Black Christmas*. That year's screening was significant, since Mom first brought me to see it when I was eleven, after much begging. It was my first big-screen horror experience and it made an indelible impression. I can still see the hippies trembling in the seats in front of us, their long hair obscuring my child's-eye view. The darkly comic thriller is about a lunatic who crank-calls foulmouthed sorority sisters from their attic, and then kills them one by one before they leave for the holidays. The first victim gets smothered with a plastic dry cleaner's bag. I sometimes photograph a friend gasping under plastic for the party invitation. I guess I'm still not over Halloween when Christmas arrives.

"We should just cancel," I pleaded, looking Mom straight in the eye that still opened a little.

"Don't be a party pooper! Just use me for this year's invitation. I need a bag over my head right now anyway, and people will think I'm wearing murder makeup."

Who was I to argue?

Indeed, friends who received the last-minute Evite replied that they were impressed by the realistically bloody bruises. Doc Holliday and his boyfriend John knew the real story, but I didn't share the news with everyone for fear they'd think the party would be a downer. A recent PETA hire, Heather, came with her dad. He was visiting from Iowa, anxious to meet her friends and colleagues. Perry opened the door to greet them, plastic bag in place (I had punched in breathing holes). The Iowans reacted with perplexed yet polite expressions as the Christmas lights twinkled on the porch behind them.

I was too distraught to bake the usual Tofurky. But we were not without sustenance. My friend Jenny made mushroom walnut pâté, John brought Silk Nog spiked with brandy, and Mom shared her oxygen mask with my silly waiter friend Eric as we giggled at the holiday classic.

Chapter 4

SNOWBOUND

"Humor keeps the elderly rolling along, singing a song. When you laugh, it's an involuntary explosion of the lungs. So, you laugh, you breathe, the blood runs, and everything is circulating. If you don't laugh, you'll die."
—Mel Brooks

In the lead-up to the New Year, as restless Perry recuperated from her yuletide wounds, I insisted we have a low-key holiday week at home. Mother Nature helped with these plans by blanketing southern Virginia with a foot of snow the day after Christmas. Mom loved watching the blizzard transform our street into a Victorian winter wonderland through the tall front windows. She also knew better than to set one pink toenail onto the porch. She would have slid down the steps faster than a Matterhorn bobsled.

Finally, we were able to chill out and settle into our new domestic arrangement. I opened a box of Crackleflame logs, and we became snowbound couch potatoes. I quickly learned that the first adjustment to living with someone who is nearly deaf is that you no longer watch TV. You watch the subtitles. No matter how hard you try to follow the action on-screen, your eyes cannot help but fixate on the text flashing below.

Mom and I made a game of catching mistakes. When Hillary Clinton referred to "the greatest nation" in a campaign speech, the subtitles read "the great estrogen." In a gladiator movie, when an ingénue told a lover he was "romantic," it appeared on-screen as "you are Roman dick." When a cross-dresser referred to RuPaul as his "Fairy Drag Mother," it read "Ferry Drag Mother," as if there had been a tragic family boating accident. I long to meet a professional subtitler to learn if these errors are the result of a faulty automated system, or if technicians actually enter joke words on purpose to amuse themselves and the hard of hearing.

Among the gifts I had put under the tree for Mom were DVD boxed sets of her favorite offbeat comedies, *Benny Hill* and *Mary Hartman, Mary Hartman*. I had the ulterior motive of a parent who parks their kid in front of a Disney marathon so they can do chores.

First, we savored a skit in which Benny plays a dimwitted talk show host unaware that the old actor he is interviewing has died in his seat. Then we howled at the episode of *Mary Hartman* in which a sick neighbor drowns facedown in the bowl of soup Mary made to make him feel better. Rewatching the scenes we first enjoyed on late-night TV when I was a child, I realized how thoroughly Mom had tutored me in black comedy. Back then,

I couldn't have imagined how gallows humor would bring such relief as I helped Mom face her own death. Laughing about the inevitable brought us the peace of mind others seek in prayer.

Refilling our coffee mugs, I left Mom to binge-watch on the couch. Then I headed upstairs to catch up on some writing in my sunny yellow office nook. It's the smallest room in the house. All that fits is my antique lift-top writing desk and a boxy wooden seat that resembles an electric chair. Since there is no door, I obscured the corner alcove behind a red, floor-to-ceiling string curtain. The tight space forces me to focus.

During the holidays, I peer into the year ahead and ponder which timely subjects will not likely receive attention. Then I plan a freelance article or two. For instance, in 2002, I figured that nobody would cover the tenth anniversary of Lawrence Welk's death. A little research showed that on the same week Welk died in 1992, *The Golden Girls* went off the air and Johnny Carson retired. Since then, TV has become so youth obsessed that elderly characters are barely visible. I pitched a story about it to *TV Guide* called "The Day the Muzak Died"—which the editors quickly agreed to publish, though they retitled it "Senior Citizens Discounted."

Mom hated my Welk obsession. To her, the show's carefree musical numbers and permagrinning cast represented everything that was wrong with her generation. I treasured the camp value and never missed a Saturday evening rerun. On PBS Norfolk, the age-appropriate sponsor was H. D. Oliver—a local funeral home.

Our usual routine went like this: Mom would holler, "Watch that shit upstairs!" I would reply, "Keep it up and I'll have you processed at H. D. Oliver so your death helps keep this shit on the air!" Then we'd smear Queen Helene Mint Julep Masques across our giggling faces and watch it together as a beauty ritual. Despite her snarky comments, Mom was proud that I was a published Welk expert, especially since the tribute I wrote for *TV Guide* earned me five hundred dollars.

I have felt compelled to write since I was a kid. I trace the impulse to my mother and an alley cat. One of the first strays I brought home was a black cat with a white face. Her markings reminded Mom of Mehitabel, a streetwise alley cat character in a satirical newspaper column she had followed as a little girl. I loved the sound of it, so that became her name. Mehitabel's best friend in the series was a philosophical cockroach named Archy, who wrote a daily newspaper column chronicling their adventures. There was no shortage of roaches in our shabby apartment complex, so I started addressing them as "Archy" when I nervously scooped them up with a newspaper to release outside.

For my tenth birthday, Mom found me an old *Archy & Mehitabel* anthology. I learned that Archy wasn't just a columnist, but a free-style poet who banged out cynical prose on a typewriter by jumping from key to key, using neither punctuation nor capital letters since bugs have difficulty with the shift key.

"The chief obstacle to the progress of the human race is the human race," he proclaimed.

The opinionated insect became my first literary obsession.

Since he spelled his name "archy" in all lower case, I started spelling mine "dan"—until a fifth-grade teacher demanded I use a capital D.

In the popular Depression-era series (written by Don Marquis), Archy ridiculed racism, pollution, and cruelty to animals, decades before they became mainstream causes. Half a century later, Archy's droll take on the world's woes inspired me to try my hand at issue-oriented writing. I used the hunt-and-peck method on Mom's old typewriter, as if my index fingers were sly roach antennae. The habit remains to this day.

I got my first break at sixteen, when the arty LA punk zine *Rattler* published a gloomy poem I wrote about animal experiments. After embarking on my career as a PETA agitator, I continued to write articles on weekends as a sort of moonlighting job to complement my nonprofit salary. Reflecting on the many times I ended up in handcuffs at protests, I wrote "A Connoisseur's Guide to the World's Jails" for *Details*, a popular nineties magazine. I rated lockups for food, accommodation, and hospitality—including whether officers allowed you to primp before a mug shot. The publication of that piece, which ended up reprinted by magazines in other countries, was as proud a moment for Mom as for me.

In 2000, the gay monthly *Genre* hired me to write a column called "Out on the Road," spotlighting some of the unusual people and places I encountered. It paid just a hundred dollars, but the clever editor, Morris Wiesinger, was so meticulous in his criticism that I considered the experience a workshop as much as a gig.

That column led to an offer to write my first memoir, *Committed*, chronicling my nomadic life as a merry militant in PETA's formative years. The only best-seller list it made was in Austin, but the book gained enough critical buzz to be released by small publishers in Australia and across Europe. Banksy read the British edition and sent me a sweet note via FedEx, along with a request to contribute to a guide he was compiling on guerrilla art. Of all the wild characters in *Committed*, Perry stood out as most readers' favorite—especially for her avant-garde, pro-homo parenting. The German gay magazine *Manner* even arranged for a photographer to shoot the two of us decorating a Christmas tree with vegetables for a holiday spread. Mom was ecstatic to be part of the book's underground appeal.

Ultimately, the paperback's modest success is what enabled me to afford a decent down payment on the Portsmouth house and move Perry in. Since she was the one who kick-started my literary aspirations with *Archy & Mehitabel*, it felt as though things had come full circle.

Chapter 5

ATTACK OF THE CHICKEN PEOPLE

With housework, hospitals, and holidays behind us, I was relieved to get back to work.

PETA's waterfront headquarters in Norfolk sits directly across the Elizabeth River from Portsmouth. The modern four-story building used to belong to a cruise company and has its own dock, complete with boat slips.

At first, I thought it would be fun to commute to work in a little motorboat. Then my merchant marine friend David showed me how choppy the deep, wide harbor gets. He is the chief engineer on massive transport vessels that sail to the Mediterranean—where he has picked up stray, emaciated mutts roaming near ports and transported them back to his home in Virginia Beach. David patiently helps me with mechanical issues.

"Learn how to put oil in your car before you consider a boat," he advised in his gruff Jersey accent. Luckily, unless the drawbridge is up, my car gets me to work in just fifteen minutes.

It took much longer to dig through the mountain of emails that accumulated over the holidays.

Much of my job is figuring out ways to keep animal rights in the public eye—a challenge given sensationalist news cycles. I try to keep an open mind for any potentially buzzworthy idea that crosses my desk. No matter how bizarre. One email that I almost deleted in haste after the holidays came from a New York novelty agency volunteering its services.

"We love the 'Rather Go Naked Than Wear Fur' campaign, and we have burlesque dancers who'd gladly strip for PETA in Times Square!" the agent wrote.

Oy. Since launching PETA's naked campaign, I have been approached by so many publicists, stage mothers, and inmates suggesting the newest pinup that my business card might as well read "Pimp for the Ethical Treatment of Animals." While thankful the campaign still generates headlines, I am keener to try more novel concepts. So I cruised the novelty agency's site. Their cheesy roster included "superhero strippers, Borat, Bush and Obama impersonators, plus-sized belly dancers, and a troupe of pint-sized performers who take the stage as mini-Kiss, mini-Gaga, and more."

My mom and I were both avid *Gong Show* fans. I tried to envision how one of these spunky characters might fit into a campaign. Alas, nothing came to mind. However, later that day, I heard that our best-selling T-shirt was the one featuring a cartoon of an angry baby chicken holding a sign that said, "I Am Not a Nugget." I froze for a second as the proverbial lightbulb went on in my head—although I sometimes confuse that with a flashing hazard sign.

Why not bring this cartoon to life? With marauding little people in chicken costumes waving "I Am Not a Nugget" signs outside McDonald's in Times Square.

The agent was surprised that we had no interest in the strippers, but gladly forwarded the nugget idea to his undersized ensemble. Later that week I received a response from Mike, one of the diminutive dancers:

"I'm the only vegetarian in the group, but we all talked about this and we'd be honored to participate. To be honest, it will be nice to use our act to combat cruelty of any kind. You have no idea the kind of daily abuse we get: kids chase us on the subway, idiots make jokes on the street, and the list goes on. Usually there's not much we can do to defend ourselves, so we look forward to going on the attack with PETA!"

Laura, the conscientious young staffer I asked to help organize it, wasn't sure it was such a good idea. "Won't this make us look exploitative?"

"Since they came to us volunteering as performers, I think it's okay. But let's see how Ingrid feels."

We walked up two flights to PETA president Ingrid Newkirk's office, where we petted a pair of orange cats she was fostering and took a seat.

"Thanks for raising this, Laura, and I'm sure you're not the only one who feels this way," said Ingrid in her British accent.

"Most of our campaigns offend one group or another, whether we work with a right-wing sheriff or a transgender model. Who knows how the protesting little people will be received? It's a unique opportunity to agitate for chickens, so let's go for it. I hope you understand."

Laura was swayed just enough to proceed, and grew to enjoy the project after a few exchanges with the enthusiastic troupe, for whom she found Day-Glo children's chick costumes online.

This overnight trip to New York was the first time I would be leaving Mom home alone. She didn't care about that—she just wanted in on the act.

"Don't you need a senior chicken? I'll use my cane. I want to go!"

Wherever she lived over the years, Mom had taken part in PETA protests. Now, even though she could barely walk, she still wanted to march.

"It would be a wonderful way for you to die, but at five foot three you're too tall, so I'm going to have to say no." I felt like dismissive Ricky Ricardo forbidding his wife from taking the stage in *I Love Lucy*. This was the first time I had to be parental with a parent, and it stung.

I met the dancers in a junior suite at the Paramount Hotel on Forty-Sixth Street. On the floor, an amorous couple sensuously straightened each other's red tights. A more serious man in his forties adjusted the rubber beak above his face so that he could see out of it without knocking his horn-rimmed glasses off.

"I'm Mike," he grinned, "the veggie nugget who sent the email."

I knelt down, gave my hero a hug, and thanked him profusely.

At the top of the pecking order, so to speak, was Israel, a

dynamic, well-built Afro-Latino in his fifties. He adjusted his snug, fuzzy yellow polyester jumpsuit in the mirror and flexed his muscles. In his Puerto Rican accent, he declared, *"I am super cheecken!"*

My phone buzzed in my pocket. I thought it was a text from my cohort wrangling reporters under the Golden Arches, but it was from my mother.

"Tell them to break a leg and I love them!"

"Tell her *gracias!*" hollered Israel. "Does she live with you?"

"Yes, I recently moved her in—she's seventy-eight but has no intention of slowing down."

"Que bueno!" he cheered beneath his beak. "I had to take in my mom, too. Getting old sucks, man. It's hard taking care of your parents, but if they were there for you, you gotta be there for them. We live in Spanish Harlem—where do you live?"

"Virginia."

"I just did an appearance in Virginia!" The sparkle in his eye promised a great story.

"It was at an uptight white wedding at a Richmond country club. The bride secretly hired me to hide under the big puffy train of her dress. I crawled on all fours as her father led her down the aisle. When the preacher asked the crowd, 'Does anyone object to this union?' that was my cue to jump out and scream, *'I object, it's me she loves!'*"

This had our entire posse in hysterics. I couldn't wait to share the story with Mom.

Like Mother Goose, I gathered my flock into the hotel elevator. Halfway down, it stopped and the door opened onto two uniformed army officers. When they saw they had to share the elevator with a gaggle of little people in chicken suits, their faces became as starched as their shirts. To avoid another giggle fit, we gazed at our feet. Mike, the bespectacled chicken, finally broke the awkward silence by saluting them in his slightly warbling voice.

"Thank you for your service!"

We winged it through the lobby and jumped into the pink limo we had rented. A mob scene awaited us under the flashing neon McDonald's sign in Times Square. I was delighted to see the sidewalk crammed with TV cameras and paparazzi, as well as onlookers. The angry birds popped out of the limo one by one like bingo balls onto Broadway.

"Cluck you, McDonald's!" they chanted, their irate expressions visible through the gaping beaks. Flapping "I Am Not a Nugget" signs over their heads, they stomped back and forth in front of the Happy Meal window posters. Photographers jumped around to shoot the scene from every angle. I steered Univision to the Spanish-speaking Super Chicken, and introduced CNN to the articulate bird in the bifocals.

"Chickens are scalded to death in defeathering tanks," Mike told the reporter through his mask. "If you saw how McNuggets were made you'd lose your lunch."

When the interviews were over, the commando chicks marched into McDonald's for a showdown at the counter, which they plastered with PETA stickers. Cashiers and customers alike froze in place and whipped out their phones to snap photos. One became "Image of the Day" on Headline News.

I took a picture, too, and texted it to my mother. I told her to watch CNN, and that I would be home that night on the late flight. The day was so exhilarating I felt like I could sprout wings and fly home of my own accord.

The plane landed in Norfolk. Still no reply from Mom. This was odd as she was such a rabid texter. Maybe she was napping. I walked into the house and heard the TV in her room. I walked in and was shocked to find her collapsed on the pink shag carpet next to her bed.

"What happened?" I gasped as I kneeled down.

"I have become the idiot in the commercial: I've fallen and I can't get up." She didn't deliver the line as a joke. She mumbled it. Her phone was on the nightstand next to the remote control, out of reach. I helped her up.

"I couldn't watch CNN. The channel was set to NBC when I fell. I did watch *Jeopardy*, though, and got every answer right except one."

At least she had her wits about her. Or so I thought.

"Were there any survivors from the plane crash?"

"What plane crash? I didn't hear about any plane crash, and mine landed just fine."

"No, not yours. A plane crashed right here on our street. I heard it and it was awful. But I couldn't drag myself to the door to see, and there hasn't been anything about it on the news." She spoke with total sincerity, which was unsettling.

"Mom, no plane crashed on our street; maybe you dozed off and had a weird dream. I just parked; it's freezing outside but everything is fine."

"*Don't lie to me, Danny Lee!*" she cried. "*I know what I heard!*"

Chapter 6

HER INNER JUKEBOX

Mom's mania, like an indecipherable accent, was hard to place.

Her mind was sharp enough to discuss detailed world history and late-breaking scandals on TMZ. This meant that Mom was not a standard Alzheimer's or dementia candidate. I had met many such afflicted seniors—parents of friends—and that was a much different party. She insisted that her problems stemmed from her hearing loss and showed me online articles about tinnitus causing noises in the heads of deaf people. This made an increasing amount of sense.

Mom kept her Richard Simmons *Sweatin' to the Oldies* videos going at all hours. At full volume. Even when she wasn't miming the moves in front of the screen. Often she was in a different room.

"You really love that Richard Simmons," I said one night, with more than a hint of exasperation. My bedroom is upstairs, but I could hear him cackling aerobics instructions through the hardwood floors.

"If I don't hear his voice, I hear other voices. Including mine."

"What do you mean?"

"I don't know what causes it, but sometimes I hear songs in my head, often sung by me, and I have a terrible singing voice. I can't stop it. Only the TV drowns it out."

I scheduled an appointment with an audiologist at Norfolk's Hearing and Balance Center. Just the name of this clinic made it seem like a perfect match for Mom. She was hopeful and enthusiastic and got all dolled up for the visit in a baby blue turtleneck. It was February, and with a bit of makeup, Mom felt her face was now presentable in the wake of her holiday injury. There was still evidence of it when she slept: her right eyelid remained creepily opened halfway. It looked like she was spying on me when I tiptoed into her bedroom to switch off *Mannix* at 3 a.m.

The polite doctor sat Mom in a glass-walled booth and fitted her with earphones. He then sat with me in an adjoining room, where he twisted dials and pushed buttons to play her noises at various frequencies. Mom smiled and bobbed her well-coiffed head, as if listening to the slow beat of a ballad. With her kissy pink lipstick and stagey smile, she looked like Doris Day attempting a comeback album. Afterward, she joined us in the control room.

"Your hearing is poor, but not terrible," said the specialist.

"Really?" Mom squealed.

"Yes, I think you should consider a hearing aid."

"I have tried them and I hate them. They pick up sounds like people chewing food across the table. It makes me want to throw up."

"Newer ones are much better."

"Thanks, but at this point in my life I don't really care what people have to say."

"I see. Then why are you here?"

"I thought you might know the significance of hearing a plane crash, or of the particular songs I hear myself singing."

"I'm afraid that's not my specialty." The doctor attempted to refocus the conversation on her test results, but Perry was intent on sharing her story.

"Is there anything I can do to hear the voice of a singer I like, or to hear just instrumentals?"

"Mom, he's not a DJ, let him finish what he has to say."

It was no use.

"I often hear myself singing an old spiritual, the one sung by slaves who wanted to escape by dying and going to heaven. Do you think that means I'm going to die soon?"

"I have no idea," he replied. "I'm not sure what you're talking about."

That was Mom's cue to launch into a harsh rendition of the song most played on her inner jukebox. *"Swing looow, sweet chaaariot, coming for to carry me hoooome . . ."*

A little old white woman attempting a big black baritone was the doctor's limit.

"Miss Lawrence, I'm not sure I can help you."

"Why?"

"I'm an audiologist, not an analyst. Given your questions, there is a chance your problems are more psychological than hearing related. I'd be happy to connect you with a specialist. . . ." He looked me in the eye. "If that's the case."

"A psychiatrist?" Mom barked. Her frosted lips snarled. *"Hell no, I'm outta here!"*

A few days later, I met Doc Holliday for a beer after his shift at the hospital. I updated him on our adventure at the audiologist's.

"He thinks the glitch isn't in her ears but her mind. Is there some subtle dementia test I could casually try on her?"

"One is to see if she's able to count backward from one hundred by sevens."

"I said subtle! We don't sit around playing math games."

"Well, another one is to see if she can follow written instructions."

I got an inadvertent result of this test the following week. Mom's medical bills started arriving—en masse. Each demanded payment in full, stating she was not insured.

Back in November, as she planned the move, Mom emailed me that she had filled out all the Medicaid and Medicare forms transferring her coverage from California to Virginia. As it turned out, she had mistakenly checked the box for food stamps instead of medical coverage. Accordingly, she now received $22 in food stamps—and over $15,000 in hospital bills from her falls, countless medications, and the futile hearing center visit.

"Danny Lee, I need you to sit down." She spread a pile of envelopes across the kitchen island. With her bowed head and guilty expression, she looked like an anxious child about to reveal a report card with all Fs.

I peered at one bill after another and was too overwhelmed to react. I was already beat from a long day at work. Mom was plenty upset with herself. What could I say? You reprimand a child in hopes they learn from a mistake, but a befuddled senior is different. Getting angry only makes matters worse.

I closed my eyes and took a deep breath. Inside, I was unnerved and knew this was a sign of more turmoil to come. Outwardly, I had to keep it together. I poured us each a glass of wine.

"I'm afraid the six-hundred-dollar Social Security check I get each month won't make much of a dent in these bills," she continued. "Maybe if you go to social services and tell them what an imbecile I am, they'll take pity and have some way of changing the forms."

I squirmed on the white wooden bar stool. "Good idea."

Looking at the jumble of papers, I tried to find something funny to focus on to lighten our gloomy moods. Separated from the bills was the colorful mailer from SNAP—Virginia's Supplemental Nutrition Assistance Program. I flipped through the contents.

"Meanwhile," I said with a smile, "these food stamps are burning a hole in my pocket!"

We celebrated making it through that first winter together with an EBT shopping spree at the Portsmouth Food Lion— if you can call spending twenty-two dollars a spree. We had to choose carefully, but we were able to get a week's worth of veggies, plus a value box of Goldenberg's Peanut Chews to scarf while watching the Academy Awards.

"When you and your brothers were growing up, all four of us could eat for a week on twenty bucks," Mom reflected as we veered down the cat food aisle.

She still refused to use her cane, but at the grocery store that didn't matter. Mom could steady herself by pushing the cart. This arrangement did not sit well with the cantankerous man behind us in the checkout line.

"Makin' your poor ol' mother push the cart," he grumbled. "What kinda son are you?"

SPRING 2009

Chapter 7

"ARE WE LIVING THE AMERICAN DREAM, DANIEL?"

The Tidewater region of Virginia is where subtropical and continental climates merge. Geologists call it the "Goldilocks Climate"—not too hot, not too cold. We enjoy four distinct seasons that change within days of when they're supposed to, a meteorological phenomenon at which I marvel, having grown up in the monotony of sunny Southern California. In Portsmouth, February's freezing polar blasts are reliably beaten back by tropical winds and rain in March.

In our backyard, the skeletons of trees that exposed us to neighbors during winter sprouted leaves almost overnight as spring began, cloaking our little world under a blanket of green foliage. On the front porch, bowls of food we left for old street cats drew an occasional baby opossum or raccoon. Their playful antics hypnotized Mom as she peeped out the front window. Hidden up high in the vines wrapping the columns, mourning doves, robins, and cardinals built nests, often decorated with a straggling strand of our Christmas tinsel. Each March, these glorious signs of life's renewal grew all the more poignant to us, since Mom's life was well into the deterioration phase.

We were now in our second year in the house.

The two of us stumbled recklessly through 2008. Unlike the lady in the commercial, we had fallen then got back up. After repeated visits to Portsmouth's chaotic welfare office, I found a caring social worker who not only reactivated Mom's medical benefits but also made the coverage retroactive. This enabled me to tell the nasty collection agency callers, who threatened both of us continually on our cell phones, to fuck off and resubmit the bills to Medicare and Medicaid.

The 2008 stock market crash cast a darker, lingering shadow. Having never invested in anything except a good stereo, I had trouble understanding the nitty-gritty of the Wall Street crisis. When I heard the Dow Jones had dropped 777 points, my only thought was *How odd, 777 is supposed to be the luckiest number. I got a 777 tattoo in Vegas after it came up on a quarter slot and four hundred dollars spilled out.*

Beyond the numerical irony, I didn't know what to make of the frenzied updates about securities and bonds. Then, in March 2009, after the market plummeted to its lowest point yet, the buzz was that houses had become worthless. Unlike stocks, I now actually owned a home.

To learn how this global calamity affected Portsmouth, I

talked to my astute neighbor Fred. He owned both the stately brick mansion behind us and the Commodore, the rehabbed cinema that lured so many businesses to High Street. Fred, who has a mop of white hair, is known as the "Godfather of Olde Towne"—and not just because he wears a loaded pistol on the belt of his blue jeans.

"It's rotten luck you bought when you did," Fred told me over the fence. Careful not to strain my back, I was planting rosebushes in hopes they would bloom for Mom's eightieth birthday in June. Fred was fixing up his Jacuzzi for the season. "Nobody knew the crash was coming, but if you had waited a year you'd have gotten your house for half the price."

"Good to know," I seethed.

"One thing you can do to bail yourself out is get a new mortgage now that interest rates are rock-bottom." Fred's wise little eyes blinked behind thick glasses. He spoke in a classic Tidewater accent, more subtle than a southern drawl. House was "hause." Since Fred was talking finance, it all sounded like Swahili to me.

"You need to renovate a bit in order to get a higher property value assessment. Then you should qualify for a mortgage that could be five hundred dollars a month less than what you're paying now."

I slowly started to comprehend. Sadly, my maxed-out credit made any significant upgrade unlikely. Then Fred imparted the most disturbing news.

"You and I love it here, but Portsmouth is not a popular residential destination like Virginia Beach. It could be ten years before our hausing market rebounds enough for your place to be worth what you paid for it. Because of when you bought, you are underwater, meaning you owe more on your place than it's worth. At least you and your mom really seem to be enjoying it."

I froze amid the weeds near the back fence. Prior to Mom's arrival, my plan had been to sell the house as soon as she dropped and move back into a small apartment. Now I would be stuck, unable to unload the abode. And it wasn't just the mortgage that drained me. With no insulation under our thin tin roof, and drafty old rattling windows, I was paying a fortune to keep the house cool during summer and warm during winter. Mom took blood thinners, which meant she was always freezing and kept the thermostat cranked to Death Valley temperatures.

"Thanks, Fred. We appreciate it. See you soon at the theater."

Discarding my forced smile, I turned around to face the old house and my dire future. In my frayed jeans, wrinkled T-shirt, and Sunday morning bed-head, I slumped back through the overgrown yard toward our splintering, washed-out wooden back deck.

I was depressed, now oblivious to the beautiful signs of spring.

Back inside, I revived the smile. If I told Mom how precarious our situation was, she would blame herself and gush guilty tears, causing me far worse stress.

"Good morning, Mom," I said with a grin, stepping into her bedroom from the back deck. Carrying on to the kitchen with a spring in my step, I sautéed home fries, toasted rye bread, and filled our coffee mugs. We settled on the couch beneath the sun-speckled striped gauze curtains to watch CBS *Sunday Morning*.

"Are we living the American Dream, Daniel?"

"Damn right!"

Chapter 8

GENTLEMAN CALLERS

The slogan "Virginia is for Lovers" rings true. People in the Old Dominion State tend to be coupled up. To compensate for the shallow dating pool, I used to date fun out-of-towners and enjoyed long-distance romances in Miami and Portland. With my new role as caretaker of both a mother and a house, those days were done. I had to adjust my tastes to suit our needs. Instead of falling for footloose party boys who wanted to travel, I now sought men whose dream trip was to Home Depot.

Mom accused me of becoming a "house whore" but she didn't complain.

Among the first of this new breed of boyfriend was Vince, a fit Italian stoner. He replaced the rusty folding chairs out front with a glossy white wooden swing, transforming our porch from *Rose-*

anne to refined. Then there was John, an affectionate Republican speechwriter who combed vintage lighting shops with me, and then wielded wire cutters to swap out the tacky tracked kitchen lights for a cooler copper fixture. After John was dyslexic J.J. with the long blond hair. He dug up the fetid little malaria fountain in the backyard, only to find that it was a submerged rusty bathtub. He wielded a scary pickax to break it apart, then filled in the crater and planted mint for our Juleps. *Cheers.*

"This is better than HGTV," Perry gaped from the sidelines in a floppy sunhat.

"Yes," I replied. "Homo & Garden."

Perry poured my gentleman callers iced tea and doted on them like a mother in a Tennessee Williams play. Privately, she warned, "You mustn't confuse your calendar and accidentally invite over more than one at a time."

Before we knew it, we were the appreciative inhabitants of an increasingly stylish home, more chic than shabby—though we had a long way to go before getting a new appraisal.

"Please try to pick up someone who can help with my computer," Mom pleaded. Although her boxy old PC worked, it had major kinks. I'm as useless with technology as I am with finance, but Perry didn't want me spending money on an unknown nerd, as she worried we'd get ripped off. Someone would come along.

The first townie I went out with for any length of time was Kevin, a clean-cut produce manager at Food Lion. He was Catholic, freshly out, and bashful—but not too bashful to venture after church to the wet underwear contest, where he stripped off his Sunday best to shake what God gave him and win four consecutive

Wet & Wild titles. I had seen him shimmy in his skivvies at the bar, but we never spoke until I was stocking up at the supermarket. I almost didn't recognize him in his neck-to-knee grocer's apron.

"Can I help you find something?" He smiled.

"Good Lord, it's *you*! With clothes on!"

He shushed me and glanced around self-consciously. "My name's Kevin."

"I'm Dan," I said, toning myself down. "I'm also a veggie—and you've got a great selection here, but I don't see any red cabbage."

"We're out of that, but I can let you know when it's in."

We swapped numbers, and a few days later Kevin called.

"The cabbage is here! How about I bring it over?"

You could've knocked me over with a piece of parsley.

That very evening, Kevin strode up and rang the bell lugging a big basket overflowing with not just red cabbage, but vegetables of every color and variety. The cost of this cornucopia would have far exceeded Mom's twenty-two dollars in food stamps.

"I've gotta be honest," he said, grinning. "I'm new to this. I've only ever hooked up with a few guys I met online or at the bar. This is my first real date. I know you're supposed to bring flowers, but I thought maybe you'd like veggies instead."

Perry was in the den glued to *Monster Truck Jam*. When she realized we had a visitor she shuffled to the hallway.

"Hi!" she said graciously. "I didn't know the grocery store delivered—how wonderful!"

"Mom, this is Kevin; Kevin, this is Perry." My eyes widened as I smiled in order to make Mother aware that this was a *special* delivery.

"*How nice to meet you,*" she cooed. She took the hint and gave him a kiss on the cheek. Mom closed the door, and behind his back gave two thumbs-up.

So began a sizzling spring fling. Kevin's apartment served as an occasional refuge, and when he came over, he patiently helped Mom with her computer. He was no technician but had enough experience from sex sites to detect a few viruses. *Phew.*

Alas, after a few months of dinners, dancing, and movies, it was evident that my romp with the grocer had an expiration date.

"I'm glad to have finally dated someone," he said. "But now I want to date others."

I was crestfallen. Not because I thought we were destined to live happily ever after, but because he was such a delightful diversion from my mama drama. Kevin was just finding himself, so it was not difficult to let go. I was sad to lose the companionship—but even sadder that I could no longer joke, "I'm dating a produce manager but he sure knows what to do in the meat department."

On Friday nights, the place to be was the Rainbow Cactus. It was a truly mixed club. Straight and gay, old and young, black and white, Latino and Asian, military roughnecks and transgendered twerkers. Most gay bars cater to men, but the Cactus overflowed with lesbians, too, from toned surfer girls to tractor tossers from Pungo.

At midnight, the dance floor was cleared for a few drag numbers, followed by Friday's big draw: the Wheelchair Drag Race. In this competition, the hosting queen placed two tipsy contestants side by side in wheelchairs at one end of the dance floor.

When signaled, amid whistles and yelps, the rivals rolled themselves as fast as they could to the other side. There, a giant pile of accessories awaited. Each would pull on a dress, step into heels, fit on a wig and a hat, grab a purse, and then plop into the wheelchair and speed back across to the finish line. The crowd cheered as if it were a NASCAR Cup race. As the contenders were often enlisted men and butch dykes, neither with much experience donning women's wear, it was a riot to watch.

I hung out at the end of the bar to get a good view of the race and joke with Fred and Kas, a bartender couple I knew. Fred was half-black, half-white, all muscle, and no hair; Kas was half-Thai and half-Irish, with a big heart and bifocals that accentuated her intelligence. By day, Kas was a nurse and Fred was a vet tech. I tried to lure him to work at PETA's mobile spay clinic, but he and Kas lived forty-five minutes away in North Carolina and already had long commutes.

One night I invited the couple over for a beer after their shift at the Cactus. Mom was a night owl, and on weekends, she was eager to meet any after-hours visitors I might bring home. I once brought in a pair of deaf hairy hillbillies with whom Mom sat up scribbling jokes and cackling long after I went to bed. When Fred and Kas drove over, I arrived twenty minutes before and gave Mom a heads-up. Like down-market Martha Stewarts, we lit candles, shoved onion rings in the oven, and had cans of Modelo on coasters by the time they walked through the door.

"Welcome!" said Mom. "Aren't you both *gorgeous*!"

"Good to meet you. I can't believe you're up!" replied Fred. When he leaned down to hug her he looked like a heavyweight boxer embracing a knitting champ. Kas kissed Perry hello and complimented her on her short turquoise nightie. I put out plates with the baked rings and BBQ sauce, and the four of us had a swell soiree in the wee hours around the kitchen island.

For a deaf recluse, Mom held her own in social situations. One on one, she could read lips, but that was difficult in a group conversation. In groups, to keep from asking *What?* repeatedly, she learned to launch into little monologues to display her wit and wisdom. She often prattled about a weird story she had seen in the news.

"Did you hear about that British Lord who painted a giant penis on the roof of his estate?" Mom asked. "Google Earth just put out a photo and Parliament is demanding he paint over it! I love it! Danny, shall we paint one on our roof?"

Our late-night visitors were charmed. As Kas was a nurse, Mom showed off her faint, year-old facial scars from the elevator fall. As Fred worked for a vet, she had him crouch down onto the pink carpet next to her bed to say hi to Daisy and Sydney, who always hid underneath. They were visible only by the glow of their timid eyes.

Finally, Mom gestured to her desk. "Do either of you know anything about computers?"

"I know enough to tell you to replace that old piece of junk!" laughed Kas. Fred nodded in agreement—but he was also deep in thought.

"Oddly enough," he said, "my ex-roommate has a decent Dell in our shed he said we could get rid of. It's not brand-new, but it's a big step up from this. You want it?"

"Are you kidding me?" Mom sputtered with excitement.

"Not at all—why don't you both come for an early dinner next Sunday and pick it up? It's Easter. We're not very traditional but we'd love to have you."

For a rare moment, Perry was speechless. New friends, a new computer, and a North Carolina Easter invitation—all at three in the morning.

The following Sunday afternoon was Technicolor blue, cloudless, and cool. Perry sported the lemon turtleneck and floral skirt we picked out at TJMaxx. She got her hair and nails done at the Vietnamese salon. I wore white jeans and a pea green western shirt. Once in the car, we meandered out of Olde Towne with the windows open for a whiff of the freshly blooming wisteria vines and magnolia trees.

As soon as we were on the country highway leading to North Carolina, I put on a soothing Bobbie Gentry CD. I was psyching myself up to share more details with Mom about Fred, his old roommate, and the computer.

"I'm so glad you finally met Fred, he's such a sweetheart," I said in my loud car voice so that she could hear.

"He sure is—and Kas, too," Perry replied, admiring the long bushy rows of peanut plants whizzing by.

"Just so you know—the ex-roommate Fred mentioned was technically a roommate—but more specifically his cell mate."

"Oh," she said, not really paying attention.

Several seconds passed.

"His cell mate?!"

"Yes. Fred was paroled a few years ago, but his cell mate is still doing time, for quite a while I'm afraid. Don't say anything, but I thought you'd like to know."

"*What was Fred in for?*"

"Grand theft auto."

"*Oh shit! He didn't hurt anyone, did he?*"

"No. He used to run with a rough crowd and got caught up in their shenanigans, including stealing a car for a wild road trip. He was arrested in Texas, trying to drive it into Mexico!"

"*Poor guy,*" she said, pondering the matter. "I love Mexico. We'll have to buy him a margarita."

We drove along without saying anything for a few minutes.

"*Wait!*" Mom exclaimed. "What about this computer? Is it hot?"

"I don't think so. It belonged to a felon Fred befriended inside. I don't know much about him, except that he's locked up for a long time. When Fred was released, the guy asked him to close down his storage shed, and to keep or get rid of the stuff in it—including the Dell."

"*Oh, Danny Lee,*" Mom marveled. "Easter with an ex-con. Jesus would *so* approve."

The sun was low when we turned into Roanoke Rapids, North Carolina. It was the setting for the real-life 1979 union drama *Norma Rae*. When we drove into town, all the textile mills had long since closed. Now it's a blue-collar dot in a very red state, known mostly as a place to stop and pee when you're driving between New York and Florida on I-95.

Fred and Kas lived in a little white house across from a big green field, where they walked Homer the greyhound, Annabelle the bulldog, and Petunia the pig. Justin and Jonathan, Kas's sweet adolescent kids from a previous relationship, greeted us in the driveway and introduced us to the animals. Inside, Fred poured pinot noir and Kas served a delicious spaghetti Bolognese made with mock meat crumbles. They were not vegetarians, but loved cooking with the latest meat-free options they found at the supermarket.

After dinner, we chilled and chatted in the living room. Petunia affectionately pinned Perry down on the couch and licked her makeup off. Mom was in love.

"This is my kind of Easter," she said, scratching the bristly pink and black creature under her chin. "A pig in my arms and not on my plate."

When it was time to leave, Fred loaded a box with the sleek black computer into my Sidekick.

"I can't thank you enough," Mom said with a hug. Then she drew back, looked Fred in the eye, and said—pointedly—"And please tell your ex-roommate how grateful I am."

Chapter 9

IT'S NOT LAST CALL AT MY PLACE

One Friday that spring, I celebrated the end of a rough week by taking myself to see *Drag Me to Hell* at Military Circle Mall. This theater draws a crowd that hollers during horror flicks with such passion that even if the movie sucks, the experience is cathartic. Both the film and the audience were top-notch. Afterward, nerves restored, I carried on to Rainbow Cactus.

I sipped a PBR, caught up with Fred and Kas, and gawked at the Wheelchair Drag Race as usual. However, I felt lonely.

Before moving in my mother, when I had nobody to look after but myself, I was content being a social butterfly or being alone. Now that I had such overwhelming domestic responsibilities, I found myself longing for the intimacy of a deeper relationship. Not just someone to help at home, but to share the emotional burdens and offer some support. Then I considered the damaged package I had to offer. Who in Virginia would want to hitch their wagon to a frantic vegan with a bad back, a deaf mother who hears voices, and a nineteenth-century money pit with an underwater mortgage? Not to mention two hissing, antisocial cats, who guarded Perry's lair like it was a pharaoh's tomb.

I had met a few dubious prospects at the Cactus.

One, a moody tugboat deckhand who looked like Homeless Jesus, took me on a foggy sunset cruise through Portsmouth's murky industrial backwaters on his skiff. The voyage was both rancid and romantic. He had some salty charm, but he was temperamental and addicted to fishing, so I jumped ship. I awkwardly fished with my dad as a kid but grew perplexed at the glee on people's faces when they hooked a struggling creature. "That's the dictionary definition of sadism," I huffed in my premature falsetto, hanging up my rod for good.

A more hopeful candidate was a striking, goateed mechanic and practicing Wiccan. The bumper sticker on his hot rod read "My Other Car Is a Broom." On our road trip to Dollywood, where he used to perform as a clog dancer, he recited an incantation to ward off the predicted rain. The pagan rain goddess must have been listening—or maybe she was a Dolly Parton fan—as the storm clouds dissipated. Our mystical affair soon followed suit.

These and other fun but futile liaisons caused me to gravitate more toward my bartender buddies at the Cactus than the frisky clientele.

On that *Drag Me to Hell* Friday, after the wheelchair spectacle, I hugged Fred and Kas goodbye and headed home. It was a quarter past one. I was melancholy as I drove along deserted I-264, about to turn into the tunnel for Olde Towne. Just then, I remembered hearing about a grubby old gay bar in Norfolk that was soon going out of business. It was called Skip's, and I had been curious to check it out before it closed. Could I get there for last call? Would anyone be there? Was it worth the effort?

My lifelong mantra kicked in: *If in doubt, go out.*

I swerved away from the tunnel and headed into downtown Norfolk, arriving at my dubious destination fifteen minutes before closing time.

Skip's was in a grimy warehouse district. The blended aroma of smoke and mildew made my nose wrinkle. The walls were nicotine-stained, the carpet encrusted with gum. Classic Queen blasted from the tarnished jukebox while contemporary queens angled shots across a scuffed-up pool table. Scanning the room, I saw two guys I knew throwing darts. They waved me over to join them. Because darts is one of the only games I am coordinated enough to play, I accepted, grabbing a Dos Equis along the way.

After my last throw, I noticed the piercing glance of someone at the bar. Like me, he had shown up at the last minute. He had curly brown hair, sideburns, an easygoing grin, and big, friendly eyes that locked on mine. There was a flurry around him as customers ordered up before closing time, but he simply stared in my direction. I thanked the dart duo and walked over to introduce myself. The discolored Coors clock on the wall inched toward two.

"Hi, I'm Daniel—you got here just in time." In loud bars, I often introduce myself as Daniel because when the music is pounding people easily mishear Dan as Stan or Ben or another one-syllable grunt name.

"I'm Jack; good to meet you, Daniel. I was at a late movie with one of my kids. Glad I made it."

Has kids, I noted.

More than a few men I had recently dated had children from a previous sexuality. Did I have an innate taste for breeders, or were more and more people finally daring to come out? Jack was about my age, but we had lived completely different lives. He had slightly rough manual labor hands—with a ring on his wedding finger. He caught me looking at it.

"I'm legally married but we've been separated for months. I only recently came out and moved out, but I go back a lot to see the kids. There are four—two just finishing high school. It's still too sensitive for me to take off the ring."

"That's cool. You're just untangling yourself from family drama and mine just started. I bought an old house and moved in my mother."

"Wow." He laughed, surprised. His expression softened into a relieved smile. "Good for you."

"I don't know about that! I'm in over my head. I work at PETA, so it's animal activism all day, elder care at night, and housework on the weekends. My mom is pretty kooky, though we have some fun."

Before either of us could say another word, the bartender blasted our eardrums.

"Last call! Last call for alcohol!"

There was a moment of awkward silence. Jack was too cute

and interesting to let vanish so quickly. I might never see him again. What could I say?

"It's not last call at my place."

Jack followed my car through the Midtown Tunnel to Portsmouth. When we entered the house, Mom was watching *Golden Girls* in her bedroom. Thanks to Bea Arthur's booming voice and Perry's weak ears, there was no chance of her hearing us bolt the door and tiptoe up the creaky wooden staircase.

"You'll meet her another time," I whispered. "I don't want to freak you out too soon."

As I worried aloud about Mom freaking Jack out, we reached the landing, where my collection of scary clown art hangs on textured burgundy walls. This gauntlet of odd thrift shop portraits has proved more alarming to visitors than my erratic mother has. The clown collection started as a joke, with just a few items, but friends kept contributing such bizarre finds that it grew into a little exhibit. It also became a litmus test revealing who shared my perverse sense of humor—or didn't.

I lit candles on dungeon-like sconces. Jack crept past the large Day-Glo ceramic relief of a clown with snarling buck teeth and sinister, half-closed eyes—"the piece I want on my tombstone." He paused at the watercolor of an obese, guilty-looking clown hiding in a bush, as if waiting for toddlers to terrorize. Next up was the smirking clown cupping his ear and straining to hear a song. He has a red knob for a nose, which I cranked to play an off-key music box rendition of—you guessed it—"Send in the Clowns."

Jack studied each piece with calm curiosity. Did he think he had stumbled into a *Silence of the Lambs* trap and was about to bolt for the door? Finally, he spoke.

"This landing looks like a set I'd do for *A Haunting*. In fact, I have a painting at the studio that would fit right in here."

"*A Haunting*? That sounds familiar."

"It's that ghost story reenactment series on Discovery Channel. We film it in Suffolk and I do the sets and props. The painting I mentioned I did myself. I worked at a carnival one summer and my boss was a nasty old drunk. When I was bored and nobody was in line for the Tilt-a-Whirl, I did a pastel oil of him as a bald, bitter clown staring into a makeup mirror with a bottle of booze in the background. I can bring it over next time if you like."

"Yes, please."

Not only had Jack passed the Clown Alley litmus test, but he had an original to add that he had painted himself. Plus he supported himself as an artist of sorts. A smile spread across my face wider than the Joker's. Jack smiled, too, seductively. On the landing, amid the flickering candles and scrutinizing jesters, we embraced and shared our first kiss. Thus began our Harlequin Romance.

"Speaking of booze, I promised you a drink."

I led him into the second-floor sunroom. The orange walls were aglow with moonlight streaming through the plantation shutters hanging askew along the corner bank of windows. Jack took a seat on the faded red sofa, facing the night sky and the silhouettes of treetops in the park across the street. I grabbed a lone bottle from a shelf—all I had was bourbon. Jack grinned when he read the label.

"Jack Daniel's," he observed. "How fitting."

"*How random*," I laughed, pouring us each a shot. "If we were a couple that's what our friends would call us." I laughed again, awkwardly, hoping the couple quip had not sounded presumptuous.

"So, what's your story?" I asked, sitting next to him. "Are you from here?"

"I was born up in Richmond—in a convent of sorts."

"No wonder you have an affinity for scary things."

"I was adopted—a few times. But I don't want to get into all of that now. I don't want to freak *you* out."

"That doesn't bother me. My mom grew up in multiple foster homes and orphanages."

"Really? One of my people. I hope to meet her."

"I'd love that."

"You sorta winced at the bar when you told me you moved her in, but I find that refreshing. One issue I've had with the gay scene is that a lot of the guys I've met lead pretty self-indulgent lives. Detached from family responsibilities. Don't get me wrong— I like to party, too, but I find you attractive because you don't seem to be living just for yourself. You have your mom, you work for animals. . . ."

Jack caught me off guard. Like the Good Time Charlies he described, I too was wary of family burdens until quite recently. And, while out on the town, I often glossed over the grim aspects of my anti-cruelty work in order to give my mind a rest—and to avoid being a Debbie Downer. It was rare to meet someone who embraced both obligations so warmly.

We talked for hours with the easy rapport of high school friends catching up after years apart.

As it turned out, Jack spent his teenage years in Orange County, California, just a few miles away from where I grew up. We bodysurfed at the same beaches, loitered at the same malls, and pogoed at the same punk clubs. He had moved to Virginia Beach with his wife and kids in the late 1990s, at about the same time I relocated to the area with PETA.

"It's crazy we've never met before, here or in California," I said.

"Well—we almost met once."

"When?"

"Years ago in Norfolk, when I worked at Showcase, that warehouse for odds and ends scrapped by restaurants and department stores. Producers shopped there for set pieces and enlisted my help—that's how I got into production design. Anyway, you came in with a friend who was buying mannequins."

"Jeez," I sighed. "That was Joey. He used to make Christmas cards posing with mannequins he dressed up like they were his family."

"The two of you were hilarious, putting the mannequins into erotic positions and joking around. You were obviously gay but didn't care what anybody thought. It made a big impression. You were free—and I was envious, being so closeted and self-conscious. We didn't speak that day but I always hoped to see you again. That's why I was staring earlier."

"Unbelievable." We stretched out and made out on the couch. Peeking out the window, I expected to see a shooting star. It must have been close to sunrise when I walked him out. We made a date to rendezvous the following evening to see a friend's band in Norfolk.

That first date lasted five minutes.

"I'm so sorry, I can't stay," Jack panted after walking in, frazzled. "My ex is losing it. I mentioned over the phone that I was coming here and she's on her way. She wants to see what I'm up to since moving out. She can get pretty hotheaded so it's best that I just leave. I wanted to tell you in person so you didn't think I flaked. I'll call sometime soon."

"Damn! Okay, don't worry." I was disappointed but wanted to be supportive. And fair. "She's entitled to rant and rave, it's all new to her, too. She might just want to see that you're not with another woman—or a guy half her age. If you ever tell her about me, be sure to say I'm a year older!"

Jack made his exit like Speedy Gonzales. I imagined whiz-bang sound effects. My friend Roderick, the mop-topped singer of the band that was setting up, saw us chatting and walked over. I explained Jack's marital drama and he shrugged. "I'm glad you got with him last night, 'cause you'll never see that guy again."

Chapter 10

PAIN LADDER

Arriving home late, I was about to open the front door when I saw a dim, distorted image of my mother through the beveled glass. She was at the base of the staircase perched on the gossip bench— a tiny chair and desk set meant for lengthy phone calls in the olden days. For a moment, I thought she might be reading, but the lights were off. She was sitting in the dark in her beige lace nightgown.

I entered and found the house uncharacteristically silent. No TV was roaring in the background.

"How are things?" I asked Mom in the shadows.

"Fine," she replied, detached. "I couldn't sleep because the kids keep running up and down the stairs. They don't mean anything by it, they're just playing. I thought I'd sit here and talk with them."

"There aren't any kids here, Mom."

"Come on, Danny." She smiled wearily. "You know better than that. It's the ghosts of kids. I think they lived here before and just wanted to visit."

"Could be," I said. She must have had another nightmare. "It seems they've stopped now. Why don't I walk you back to bed?"

Mom shuffled along without complaint. She gulped a pill. I tucked her in and kissed her good night. Then I made a beeline for the foyer to sit on the gossip bench myself. I tried to keep both my mind and ears open for any stomping young phantoms. The only noise I heard came from crickets.

I always wanted to believe in ghosts, but none had ever so much as said "Boo," despite my earnest attempts to make contact. Before this house, I lived around the corner in a stately building that had served as a hospice during Portsmouth's yellow fever epidemic of 1855. Thousands perished—many in the very room I had rented. Because so many fever victims had died right where I lived, I always hoped to encounter a spirit. Alas, none ever materialized, even when I lit candles, broke out the Ouija board with superstitious friends, and set the tone by playing Peggy Lee's "Fever."

Having witnessed no spectral brats on the stairs, I trudged up and brushed my teeth. Before turning in, I checked on Mom. Fortunately, she was sound asleep. The only thing stirring was the candle atop her dresser, which flickered shadows on her drug shrine—an actual altar, complete with rosary beads and candles.

Mom placed her pill bottles like votive offerings around a ceramic bust of Jesus Malverde, Mexico's patron saint of drug runners. Legend has it that in the early 1900s, the dapper bandito funneled drug money to the poor. Since his death, makeshift memorials to the outlaw appeared in the Mexican state of Sinaloa—and on my mother's cedar dresser in Portsmouth. She intended it more as an homage to a folk hero than a prayer tableau, though I once overheard her standing at the shrine and talking to Jesus (the dealer, not the Savior).

Some of Mom's meds helped her failing heart and lungs: blood thinners, beta-blockers, inhalers, antibiotics, and diuretics. She also took thyroid pills and several vitamins. Of more concern was her expanding collection of painkillers to dull the ache of chronic arthritis. Mom loathed the stupor caused by most opiates, so whenever she saw a doctor she asked for the newest narcotic in hopes of finding one that worked for her. Physicians dutifully wrote one prescription on top of another. This was the formative era of the opioid epidemic—years before overdose deaths had become big news, and nearly a decade before the crisis was declared a national emergency.

Mom was amusingly aware of her dependence on drugs and the side effects, which she continually researched online. When she read that a steroid she took might be responsible for her angry outbursts, she changed her email address to MsRoidRage@hotmail. After learning that another capsule she downed could cause paranoia, she began signing her emails "Perry Noid."

As I stood before the luminous display of drugs, it occurred to me that one of the mystery meds—or a combination—might be causing Mom to imagine voices and sounds, and to lose her balance. After all, the hearing specialist had ruled out tinnitus. The next morning, I called Doc Holliday and listed the prescriptions.

Many were old, from California, others from the Richmond ER, and still more from a general practitioner I brought her to in Norfolk.

"You listed four different painkillers," Doc gasped. "That's bad—they compete with each other and overwhelm a body that's already weak. This happens a lot with seniors. Ask her to pick one and cut the rest immediately."

Mom trusted Doc's assessment, but she was flustered.

"I have no idea which painkiller to choose. I've mingled them for so long I don't know what works anymore. Some of the other meds make me loopy, too. This will be very difficult to figure out. What do you take for your back pain, Danny? Maybe I should take that."

"I couldn't stand any of the painkillers prescribed for my back. They made me comatose and unable to function at work. I just ice it and take anti-inflammatories, which don't help much."

"What does David take?" Mom asked. She was referring to my gardener friend in Washington. "He must take pain meds for the yard work he does every day. He said he was starting to get arthritis."

"David smokes pot. Otherwise he's like me, he can't pop those pills and work all day in a catatonic state."

"Well, that makes you two the perfect control group! Candidates for pain meds who aren't on any! You guys test each pill and tell me which one is the keeper."

"Are you the same mother who forbade doctors from giving me Ritalin as a child? I hate pharmaceuticals. I can't even watch the asinine commercials."

"I know, but I have to take some of that crap! I cannot live in pain. Come on, Danny. I'm an old lady and I've been dosing for years—you and David are sturdy guys, one pill won't hurt you. And it's not like you two are strangers to stimulants."

She had a point. She once heard us reminiscing about mushrooms and exclaimed, "You never ate mushrooms as a kid."

"That was before he tried the magic kind," David informed her.

David and I have been close since we lived on the same dorm floor at American University in the 1980s. He had bonded with Perry when she visited us there, and their own separate friendship took root. Another loner adopted by Mom: this one an irreverent New Jersey Jew with a shaved head, tattoos, and an obsession with female vocalists of the 1940s. David established a successful landscaping business in our nation's capital, where he manicured the lush gardens of Georgetown mansions. He spent occasional holidays with Perry over the years, helping her make the most of the little plot of dirt outside whichever apartment she rented. Now that spring had arrived, he was planning to hoe it up in our raggedy backyard. I called and explained Mom's pill proposition.

"Is this a job for us?" I asked. "Maybe it'll be like our senior trip. Only a different type of senior and a much different trip."

"Oh, *Dan*." David deadpanned. "I don't know. I do love Perry and want to help, but . . . let's figure it out when I get there."

The following Friday, David drove his pickup three hours south to rainy Portsmouth. After a pleasant catch-up dinner with Mom, he and I retreated upstairs to the orange room and got to work—first with a little research.

When we Googled "opiates" one of the first things to come up was the WHO's Pain Ladder. I thought we had stumbled upon a 1960s rock site. Clicking the link, we learned it wasn't the band the Who, but the World Health Organization. Pain Ladder wasn't a song, but a ranking of painkillers and their traits. Bingo. The four Mom took were on the middle and top rungs. They all produced various levels of delirium and loss of balance.

"I bet one of these caused Mom's falls," I told David, flashing back to Perry's horrific, skull-shattering ER episodes. "They could be causing her delusions, too. She can't live like this, and neither can I. Shall we help with the process of elimination and be done with it?"

David agreed. We planned to take a different sedative each morning and evening, spaced apart the suggested six hours so we could gauge their distinct impact. I have never had such a sedate weekend, and I never will again. At least the beating rain made it feel cozy inside.

On Saturday morning, breakfast consisted of bananas, cashews, and Darvocet. We were intrigued, as the substance had been banned in Europe. The single dose we took wasn't enough to cause side effects like itching and sore throat. However, it made the blood coursing through our veins feel like cement.

We were immobilized, too sluggish to flip through the illustrations in the *Kama Pootra* book David brought ("52 Mind-Blowing Positions for Pooping"), and too bewildered to follow the plot on *The Partridge Family*. Hell, we couldn't even sing along to the theme song—"C'mon Get Happy"—which made us angry, not that we could express that emotion, either. This drug went right onto the discard list. Maybe Mom was on it when she screwed up her Medicaid forms. I wasn't surprised when the Food and Drug Administration banned it a few years later because so many users had committed suicide.

Our big date for Saturday night was with a pill that went by the name Gabapentin. This drug drew David's interest as it was prescribed not just for pain but to help you quit smoking and make you more at ease in social situations. We were also curious to see why it was among the most popular drugs smuggled by California prison inmates. Alas, like Darvocet, this dope got two thumbs-down. Taking it was like having a pause button pushed on your life; we were trapped in a state of suspended animation. It probably helped fight smoking because lifting a cigarette would be a herculean task. The only social gathering it could make you feel acceptable at is a funeral. We slumped on the couch and watched—what else—*Valley of the Dolls*. On this drug, even that psychedelic pill-popping camp classic didn't elicit the laughs it usually did. Who could live anaesthetized like this all the time?

"On the seventh day he rested." *Not me*. Come Sunday morning I was jonesing to get active. Fortunately, Klonopin was not nearly as deadening as the previous meds. It even gave us an intoxicating sense of bliss. The sun was finally shining so we poured ourselves coffee and sat on the porch swing. We were mesmerized by the sharp-eyed birds tweeting and fluttering in the trees above, and by the aloof power walkers tweeting and tripping on the street below. The church bells rang. David and I took this as a call to get out of the house.

We walked in a daze alongside stragglers who were heading to the early service at Monumental Methodist. Though the church was built in 1831, the motivational messages on the changeable letter sign out front were always up to date. Since the recession had just hit, it read, "We have a prophet-sharing plan." During a heat wave, it was "This church is prayer-conditioned." Vandals once covered up letters on the display case, rechristening the church "Monumental Meth." I recounted this to David as we stumbled past in a drug-induced giggle fit.

We carried on to Olde Towne Coffee Shoppe but did not go inside. Standing near the entrance was the Olde Towne Crier—an eccentric local dressed as a colonial aristocrat, complete with wig and tricorn hat. In an English accent, he bellowed proclamations about the farmer's market, the weather, and what-have-you. On this morning, he did not get past "Hear Ye! Hear Ye!" before David looked at me in a panic. "I can't handle this right now, let's go home."

Walking back, we felt disoriented on the warped sidewalk. We almost tripped in potholes where bricks were missing. Despite the pleasant sense of euphoria, Klonopin can make you dizzy and unsteady. Maybe it caused Mom's gory falls. Onto the reject pile it went.

Last up for Sunday afternoon was Vicodin. By that point, we had decided to split a dose. Like Klonopin, it made us feel good rather than dead, and we were functional. We played Scrabble with Mom. I cleaned the house. David worked in the backyard, planting the weeping willow sapling he had brought. This medicine went down easily. At least initially. I can see why it crept up to become such a popular monster in the opioid crisis.

"Vicodin is the one," David announced to Perry in front of her drug shrine. "But half a pill goes a long way. The rest are terrible!"

"I can't thank you enough!" Mom cooed, hugging us both. She grabbed the other little bottles from the base of the Jesus Malverde bust and handed them to me. "Danny, put these out in the trash under the dirt from David's yard work. I'm glad to be rid of them."

Under the covers in bed that night, I felt euphoric. Not from the smorgasbord of tranquilizers, but from the sense that we had likely eliminated the painkillers causing Mom's dizziness and near-fatal falls. I closed my eyes and said a little prayer to Jesus Malverde that we had also rooted out the drug behind the voices and delusions plaguing my mother.

Chapter 11

A COSMIC HAPPENING

There was an early exodus from the PETA office as people lined the harbor to witness the rise of the giant dazzling supermoon. I had planned to take in the rare astrological event with Mom at the Portsmouth marina. On this clear, balmy evening, the full moon would rise closer to the earth than it had been in decades, making it appear one-third bigger and much brighter than normal, almost like a sun. I had just gotten into my car when Jack called. A few weeks had passed since we met.

"I was driving home thinking about you and missed the turn for Norfolk," he said. "Now I'm heading toward Portsmouth. My hands are instinctively steering me in your direction. Are you free?"

"Sure! The supermoon is coming. Meet me on the patio of the Deck. It's the restaurant in the middle of the marina."

Portsmouth's marina is home base for hundreds of local boaters and a big draw for those sailing up and down the East Coast. It's Mile Marker Zero on the Intracoastal Waterway, a series of rivers and canals that flow from Portsmouth all the way to the Florida Keys, an inland passage safer for small ships than the open ocean. The Deck is where pleasure cruisers gas up, stock up, and drink up before embarking on the journey. On this celestially significant evening, the place was hopping.

I was lucky to score an outdoor table just before Jack arrived. The slowly setting sun bounced off the river and made us glow as we sat across from each other sipping Shock Tops.

"I don't really know what to say," he began apprehensively. "I've been living a lie for so long I'm not sure how to sound sincere. Basically, I'm still working out my past, but I hope you'll be part of my future."

Jack started to reach across the table for my hand but grew nervous and stopped short. Instead he extended a stealthy leg and gave my foot a tap. Like him, I was hooked but uneasy. He was just shedding a marriage of nineteen years. The worst thing for him would be to jump into another intense relationship. I had made similar mistakes with guys who had been married a fraction of that time.

"Count me in," I replied. "But don't put yourself under any pressure. I don't want this to be a white-hot affair that crashes after a few months because you never enjoyed some freedom. While you were raising four kids, I had forty boyfriends. You should experience the gay life you were always curious about. Sleep around, date different people, figure out what you like. If that turns out to be me, I'll be delighted. Right now you need a good friend, and so do I. Shall we be friends—well, friends *plus*—and see how it goes? Keep in mind I have domestic problems of my own: a run-down mother with a house to match."

"*Deal!*"

As the sun continued its descent, my phone buzzed. It was a text from Mom, who had just swallowed her evening Vicodin: "The full moon is coming and I'm fully medicated. Where are you?"

Jack leaned in. "Is it your turn to cut the date short?"

"Not necessarily." I read her text aloud.

Jack laughed. "Looks like we have a chaperone."

We picked Perry up in Jack's Land Rover. I had already told her all about him, and she eagerly awaited us in front of the house with a bulging purse.

"Hi, Jacky!" Mom squealed as I helped her into the front seat. "Wonderful to meet you!" She leaned over, charm bracelets rattling, and gave him a hug and a kiss. "Now step on it before we miss the supermoon. We're really into cosmic happenings."

"Me too," he beamed. Perry was unable to stretch her seat belt around her mega-purse, so Jack reached over and clicked it into place.

"I've heard so much about you," Mom continued. "Good for you for going gay when your marriage ended. If only I'd had it in me to become a dyke after my first divorce, it would've saved husband number two a lot of grief. But then of course we wouldn't have Darling Danny Dimples here or his brothers. . . ."

I was both mortified and amused—the usual mélange of emotions whenever I introduced Mom to a suitor. I wanted to interject but it was no use. She had already launched into one of her monologues. Jack took it in with a grin as he navigated us back to the waterfront.

"It's *thrilling* that you are in show business. I want to see pictures of your sets. Keep in mind that I'm available for extra work, though I'm too deaf to hear it when the director calls *Action!*"

We were back in the marina parking lot in minutes. We had just enough time to walk out to the Deck before sunset. Only Mom didn't want to hobble down the crowded floating walkway to the restaurant.

"This car is *sooo* comfortable. Let's watch the supermoon from here." She reached into her purse and pulled out cans of diet grape soda for each of us, followed by a package of Red Vines, which she tossed to me in the back to open. Arthritis had made it impossible for her to pull apart the plastic wrapper. I passed out the licorice while we peered impatiently at the dark river stretching out before us, as if Godzilla might surface. Jack inched his car to the edge of the dirt lot overlooking the water for an optimal view. Mom pushed a button on her armrest in an attempt to open her window, but nothing happened.

"That's the seat warmer," Jack said, smiling.

"Really? I've never had my seat warmed." As her seventy-nine-year-old butt got toasty, Mom started moaning and swaying. She looked like Barbara Bush demonstrating a lap dance. "*Ooh, this is heaven. I'm never leaving this car.*"

I grimaced in the backseat. Jack chuckled, turned to me, and said, "I see where you get your lack of inhibition."

A din of applause echoed from the marina.

"There it is!" I shouted. The supermoon looked like a radiant sun emerging from the depths of the wide harbor along the horizon.

"It's like *Close Encounters*," Mom yelped.

The glimmering disc soared like a meteor through the starry cobalt sky. Perry pulled out her camera and took pictures through the windshield, none of which came out because the flash bounced off the glass. Careening sharply, the supermoon was soon obscured by the spires of one of Portsmouth's grand churches.

"*Goddamn churches always getting in the way!*" shouted Mom.

Our lunar odyssey was an otherworldly icebreaker and the genesis of an unexpected family unit. Jack started coming over a few nights a week. We had sparkling candlelit dinners in our Dusty Blue dining room.

At first, I served as the house chef. I prepared exotic entrées like bok choy and rice noodles seasoned with anise and topped with lemongrass fried seitan. Jack, new to vegan cuisine, was shocked by the flavors, weird greens, and meat analogues I found at the Chinese and Indian grocers. He was wary of the most potent spices but overall was fascinated. He had previously only tried tofu and was not a fan. Mom humored me for a while, but she was a vegan who hated vegetables. The only spices she liked were salt and pepper. She loved foreign films but hated most foreign food.

"If I had my way we'd eat sandwiches, pasta, or potatoes every night," she complained. "I am a starch queen."

"That's the kind of stuff I made for my kids," Jack admitted. "Let me see if I can fix vegan versions." He explored the stores and experimented, acing spaghetti with mock meatballs, BLTs with fakin' bacon, twice-baked potatoes with onion gravy, and—the starch queen's favorite—grilled soy cheese sandwiches. On nights when Jack cooked, Mom hovered in the kitchen with the same enthusiasm her cats displayed waiting by their food bowls in the morning.

Carbs were not all they had in common. They chatted candidly about their orphan origins. Both were conceived by accident, born with blank birth certificates, and raised by a succession of strangers. However, their stories were very different.

Jack explained how he was called Phillip as a baby among the nuns. He sat across from Perry at our old oak dining table so she could read his lips.

"A newlywed couple adopted me and renamed me Dennis, but they divorced after a year and had to give me back. Next, a military couple adopted me and christened me Jack, after my new father. He died in Vietnam. His wife Rosemary remarried and had kids of her own. I grew up with them and had a very good life, but always felt like an outsider. That's why I was anxious to marry young and have kids, to create an actual family of my own. Only to realize I was gay!"

"Oh, *honey*," said Mom, patting his hand. "That's fucked-up. No wonder you feel at home in this asylum. Did you ever meet your original mother?"

"Yes. Carol. When I turned eighteen, she tracked me down and we had a wonderful reunion. She was a teen when she got pregnant and her parents sent her away to have me at a Catholic home for unwed mothers. The experience tormented her and she wrote a book about it, called *The Other Mother*. Believe it or not, NBC made it into a movie in the nineties."

Intrigued but not wanting to interrupt, I refilled our glasses with the finest merlot that 7-Eleven had to offer.

"Did you ever know your parents?" Jack asked Perry.

"I never knew who my father was. I did get to know my mother a bit. She was an aspiring DC socialite in the Roaring Twenties. Her dream of living the high life fizzled when she got knocked up with me. She wanted nothing to do with me. I went from the hospital directly to a foster home. The same one my brother Bill ended up in a year before. We soon made the rounds to a dozen more."

Mom told Jack how during the Depression, couples got money from the state if they fostered kids. Some were a godsend but others just did it for the cash. They pledged to raise God-fearing children and got carried away with the fear part.

"We bounced from Methodists to Baptists to Presbyterians. The trait most of them had in common was scorn for other beliefs—each telling us we would burn in hell if we didn't adapt to their way of worship. Bill went along with it but not me. I questioned them, which often resulted in a beating or being sent to bed without dinner. By the time I was eight, when I was brought to any new foster home, I told them when they opened the door that I would have no part of their religion. That made me a little hard to place."

"She's still hard to place," I interrupted. "That's why she's here."

Mom giggled before flashing the one bit of sign language she knew—the middle finger.

"Eventually, our mother took us in for a few years. Bill got along with her, but she constantly berated me. Threw scalding water at me. When I turned ten, I ran off to an orphanage. It was a great haven and I loved the camaraderie. Then I got lucky with a truly wonderful foster mother, Ellen. She became my godmother, though I just called her Mama."

Perry pointed to a framed, vintage black-and-white photo hanging on the far wall. In it, Mom was a girl of twelve with a blonde bowl cut, embraced by Ellen, a gentle, dark-haired middle-aged woman with glasses.

"She was the first person to show me kindness. Those were a good few years, before Ellen passed, God rest her soul." Mom often used religious jargon despite being a heretic.

It was heartwarming to listen to Perry and Jack compare their unusual upbringings so freely. When my brothers and I were growing up, we got the Disney version. Mom told us how she skipped school to roller-skate around wartime Washington, sit in on trials at District Court, or read in the Library of Congress. In the evening, she took the streetcar to the end of the line to play with her black friends in the segregated capital. Despite our questions, we learned very little about the abusive foster homes or her unhinged mother.

"You kids have enough problems without hearing about my loser baggage," she would say.

Likewise, Jack was much more at ease sharing details about his adoptions with Mom than he had initially been with me. They developed an "orphan bond," which I learned could be just as profound as ties between blood relatives.

"When did your name become Perry?" Jack asked.

"That was much later," Mom said softly. Unsure whether she should tell the story, she averted her eyes as they began to tear up. I nodded to encourage her.

"I was raped when I was in my sixties. I was living in Arizona then. He was a rough character from Brooklyn I had recently broken up with. He stalked me in the garage by my apartment and attacked me one night."

Jack clasped her hand.

"By the time I pulled myself together and went to the police, he had fled the state. They said in the off chance he could be located and extradited, it would be a long, drawn-out case. I could not handle that, especially at that age. I just got the hell out. The kids helped me move to California and I changed my name to Perry. I always wanted a unisex name anyway."

In my mind, that gut-wrenching episode marked the moment my mother turned into an old lady. Her carefree spirit and independent nature had been devastated. She stopped working regularly and tried to rely on her meager Social Security checks, along with help from my brothers and me.

To get her mind off the ordeal, I took her on a road trip through her beloved ancestral Ireland when she turned seventy. It was a fantastic adventure. We even woke up in an ancient castle on her birthday. We did a lot of sightseeing, but she was becoming doddery. I would not have acknowledged it at the time, but that's when it first occurred to me that I might have to look after her in later years.

As spring surged in Portsmouth, so did our unlikely troika.

Mom, Jack, and I found ourselves relying on one another for emotional and physical support. I helped Jack placate his irate ex by trying to see things from her point of view. I got him to relay his feelings to her in handwritten letters rather than quarrelsome phone calls or texts. After all, they had to regain some civility before initiating a divorce. Likewise, Jack helped me deal with Mom, who could be very prickly with me, but never him. In addition, Jack's production experience made him extremely handy at home.

As the weather turned warm, he remarked how stuffy it was in the house.

"The damned AC keeps conking out," I complained. "It's frustrating. The unit is out back and the repairman says ants keep getting into the electrical box and shorting it out. I have done everything he said, elevate it off the ground, put repellent down, but it keeps breaking and he keeps coming to re-fix it. It's costing me a fortune."

Jack went out and inspected it, then fetched a tool kit from his

Land Rover. Twenty minutes later, the AC kicked on. Mom and I rejoiced and danced a jig under the vent.

"All I did was wrap the power box with electrical tape so the ants can't get in. I think the repairman was gouging you." The AC never broke again.

Chapter 12

FAMILY PLOT

Mom and her brother, Bill, in the 1930s.

The unseasonably warm weather continued that spring. One muggy Friday, Mom and I endured the heat dressed head to toe in black for a somber day trip. Her long-absent brother had died. As much as I dreaded formal funerals with distant relatives, I looked forward to this open-casket service. I thought it might finally prompt Mom to exhume more of the skeletons in her family closet.

The Lee Funeral Home in Clinton, Maryland, sits amid ugly strip malls one block from a noisy highway leading to DC. Not a tranquil place for a solemn service during the afternoon rush hour. Fumes from the traffic made the humid April air heavy and grimy. John Wilkes Booth would never recognize the town today. It was a quiet country village in 1865, when he and some cohorts on horseback regrouped at a tavern here after he assassinated Lincoln.

I pulled into the 7-Eleven across from the mortuary for some water to wash down the half a Vicodin that Mom offered to ease my piercing back pain. After the three-hour drive from Portsmouth, my lower vertebrae pinched my innards like an angry spider crab. We had a taxing day ahead of us before driving back. Next to the convenience store was a grubby sports bar.

"I hope the service ends before happy hour," I joked, stepping out of the car carefully to avoid twisting my spine. I had to yell so Mom could hear me over the rickety drone of my Sidekick's overburdened air conditioner.

"If we had any sense we'd have brought a flask," she smirked, poking the big black purse at her feet with her cane. Although she hated using the cane in public, she liked to gesture with it to dramatize a point, as if that were the sole reason she lugged it around.

Mom's brother Bill had resurfaced toward the end of his life after half a century off the radar. I had met Uncle Bill and his doting Jewish wife, Neome, only a few times. They were a loving couple in their seventies who married late in life after previous marriages. Bill was portly, affable, and meek. At any sign of discord, such as an unpleasant childhood memory brought up by my mother, he put his hands in his pockets, shifted his weight from side to side, smiled, and shrugged.

Neome was outgoing and warm. She sported dark red hair, generously applied makeup, and classy department store clothes. She could also be pushy. One night at a restaurant, for ten full minutes Neome stared down the lingering occupants of the booth we were waiting for until they paid and left. Once seated, she opened her roomy handbag and removed a pair of gold lamé bibs, which she and Bill strapped on before enjoying the linguine dinner. Afterward, Mom gabbed more about the bibs than Bill's backstory.

Would I ever learn why they hadn't spoken for fifty years?

Neome's pushiness was responsible for Mom's life-changing reunion with her brother. Shortly after they got married, Bill told Neome of a sister whom he hadn't seen since FDR was president. Neome enlisted the help of a friend who worked for Social Security to track her down. It was a difficult task as Mom had changed her name many times. After several years, they uncovered her most recent identity—Perry Lawrence—and found her address. She lived clear across the country. Mom, who had long given up hope of ever seeing Bill again, was in a state of disbelief when the letter from Social Security arrived. She immediately flew back for an emotional reunion with her brother several years before he died.

"We had a rotten start but at least things ended on a good note." Mom smiled as she applied lipstick in my rearview mirror.

Bill's funeral brought Mom close to her roots in DC, where as a child she speed-skated around the cherry blossoms each spring. Seventy springs later she limped with a cane. In place of her bright knee-high baby-doll dress were charcoal slacks and a black turtleneck. A neatly brushed bob of white hair touched her stooped shoulders. She concealed her blue eyes behind dark square shades. The only remnant of her childhood self was evident in the color she still painted her nails: Cherry Blossom Pink.

I wore a shiny black collared shirt with a thick zipper down the middle. Mom hated it.

"You look like a goddamn busboy!"

"It's boiling out and this is the coolest thing I have in black." I dragged the zipper down to my navel and leaned my chest into the AC vent. Mom took a sip of water. Finally, we made our pilgrimage through the hot parking lot to the cool mortuary.

Inside the bland all-purpose chapel, Neome held court in the front row opposite the casket. Sitting behind her was Robert, her thirtysomething son from her first marriage. He had wavy brown hair, inquisitive eyes, and a drooling mouth. When Robert was eleven, a ruptured ear infection caused permanent brain damage, which stunted his growth physically and mentally. But the part of his brain that absorbed music flourished. If there was a piano around, Robert played it like Liberace. Most of the time, he just belted songs from vintage musicals he had seen as a kid, arms whirling like a cabaret performer.

Peppering the tearful condolences mourners offered to Neome were Robert's renditions of "Mammy" and "Ink-A-Dink-A-Doo," accompanied by moves reminiscent of the "Hand Jive" number in *Grease*. Robert clapped his hands, ran his fingers through his hair, then slumped into hibernation for a few minutes until the next tune fought its way out. He was surrounded by similarly animated friends from his school, and their plus-sized nurses.

Mindful of my spine, I cautiously squatted down to hug Neome, whom I greatly admired. Overwhelmed by the intense floral aroma of her perfume, I struggled to speak without coughing.

"You're certainly holding up well."

"Thank you, Danny." Neome clutched a handkerchief. "It's all a façade."

"Please tell me if there's anything I can do to help."

A bald man leaned in and handed her a cassette. "This has all of Bill's favorite Glenn Miller songs."

"Thank you, sweetie."

Neome placed the tape in my hand and directed me to put it in the casket. Exhaling Gardenia, I stepped over to the casket, where I inhaled formaldehyde. I whispered a prayer of gratitude for Mom's painkiller. It was easing my rattled nerves as well as my backache.

Only the top half of the coffin lid was open. The first thing I noticed was that Uncle Bill's girth was gone. Not so much from his face but from his stomach, which seemed deflated. He looked like one of those cartoon characters who get flattened by a steamroller but manage to keep their three-dimensional head intact. I plopped the cassette onto Bill's chest, and instead of coming to a muffled stop, it rattled with a metallic clink. Was there a cookie sheet under his tuxedo shirt? It was disconcerting, but as mortuary makeovers go, he looked good.

Refocusing on Uncle Bill's face, I thought of how his reemergence into Mom's life had helped her let go of whatever misfortune had driven a wedge between them. I mouthed the words "Thank you." That's when it occurred to me: they didn't look much alike.

As soft organ music played, I walked to the table of photographs Mom was scrutinizing and leaned into her tin ear. "I want to hear more about you and Bill and your mother—and whoever your father was. You've still never shared the whole story."

"It's all water under the bridge; what difference does it make?"

"Come on, isn't this the time and place? I've always wondered what made your mother so bitter toward you that you bolted while Bill didn't seem to draw such a wrath. Were you a brat from hell or did something happen?"

"I've always considered Bill my brother but in fact, he's my half brother. When Bill was a toddler, our mother had a fling and got pregnant with me. Bill's father divorced her and my father wanted nothing to do with her or me. She received no help from him and only a little from Bill's dad, who told her when turning over child support, 'I don't want any of this money going for the girl.' When my mother looked in my face, she told me all she saw was the man who had ruined her life. Does that clarify things?"

"Uh . . . yes," I said, dumbfounded by the blunt explanation.

"*One by one they pass away, the Brothers of our adoption, the Companions of our choice,*" announced the white-robed Freemason at the back of the chapel as the pre-show commenced. He looked like an unhooded Klansman or an attendant at the medieval-themed buffet at the Excalibur in Las Vegas. The Freemasons, the centuries-old secret-handshake society to which Bill belonged, had organized his funeral. Masons use Gothic symbols, such as a skull and bones, which, according to bylaws, "remind us of death, the ultimate equalizer of man." Accordingly, a Mason's funeral is a big deal. Uncle Bill had a full house.

When Neome told Perry that she was expecting many of Bill's friends from the "temple," Mom assumed that her brother had converted to Judaism. But when Bill's robed brethren and their wives from the *Masonic* temple slowly filed through the door, she did a double take.

"At least it's nondenominational." Mom chuckled. We took aisle seats in the second row.

As the organ droned, my mind buzzed with questions. This may not have been the ideal setting for a heart-to-heart, but Mom seemed finally primed to open up and I didn't want to miss the opportunity.

"When was the last time you actually saw Bill all those decades ago? What happened that pulled you apart?"

"It was late one night, after my catastrophic first attempt at marriage," she whispered. "I was pregnant with no place to go. The only person I could turn to was my brother. He had also recently married—his first wife, not Neome. I was desperate and knocked on the door to ask if I could stay for a few days. Bill kept me waiting on the cold porch. He came back a few minutes later to explain, in his nervous way, that his wife was deeply religious and didn't want the stigma of an unwed mother staying in their home. That was the last time I saw him until Neome tracked me down more than fifty years later."

"How awful." I clasped her hand. "That was when you were pregnant with Timothy?" Tim was my much older half brother. We didn't know he existed until 1971, when he vroomed up to our Southern California apartment on a Harley-Davidson. He settled nearby and had two kids, Jenny and Andy, whom I babysat as an adolescent. At the time, Mom didn't discuss Timothy's origins. As far as I knew, he was a Cabbage Patch Doll who came to life and became a biker.

"No, I wasn't pregnant with Timothy then."

I was thoroughly confused.

"If it wasn't Tim, who was it?"

"Patricia." Mom's eyes teared but she remained poised.

I clammed up as the organ played a melodramatic score to this family revelation.

"I was nineteen. My first marriage had collapsed and I had no means of support. Timothy's father, Tennessee, and his family took Tim away from me. I met someone on the rebound and got pregnant with Patricia, but that man wouldn't marry me. After my brother refused to take me in, I arranged for Patricia to be adopted. I haven't seen her since. That nearly did me in."

"Oh, Mom. I'm so sorry. I wish I had known."

"I didn't need you kids or your friends or their parents thinking I was a complete failure," she whimpered, while still keeping her composure. "I didn't want to be one of those people who are defined by their problems. I have no place for pity. I just kept this to myself. And a few friends along the way."

It struck me that Mom had repeated the same tragic pattern as her mother: having two kids back-to-back by two different men and losing everything as a result. What emotional state must have driven those predicaments? As sorry as I was to hear about these ordeals, I felt a great sense of relief that she was finally opening up about it. We had always been very close, yet before today, I barely had the outline to Mom's life story.

The master Mason continued his spooky incantations in the last row. Other robed participants gradually encircled him.

"A Brother whose hand we have clasped in the bonds of Fraternal Fellowship is now passing from our sight, and we know that we shall meet him on Earth no more."

Up front, the crowd at the casket started thinning out. Among the stragglers were Robert and his classmates. Their nurses instructed them to follow the Catholic ritual of kneeling on the stool and touching the corpse. Amid giggle fits, Robert and his friends jabbed at Uncle Bill's wilted remains and then scurried back to their seats. Finally, Mom rose to have a solemn final moment with her brother.

"I'll do this alone," she said, grabbing her cane.

Soft organ music wafted through the cooled air as Mom carefully knelt on the stool. She leaned into the casket to kiss Bill goodbye.

Suddenly, Mom stiffened with a jolt. Something had startled her. She leaned farther into the coffin and put both hands in, grabbing around. She was probably fixing Bill's jacket.

A few mourners tearfully glanced at each other at Mom's poignant farewell.

She was having trouble reaching something. Maybe she was just unable to get the leverage to stand back up. She swiveled her head toward me.

"Come up here, Danny! And bring my bag!"

Must be her arthritis. I grabbed Mom's purse and rose, still loopy from the Vicodin. I didn't want to draw attention, but when a six-five man with a purse staggers to the front of a small funeral chapel, eyeballs follow.

As I approached, I saw that Mom was fumbling over her brother's corpse trying to reach a large shimmering metal crucifix, complete with Jesus figurine. Thankfully, the organ music drowned out Mom's next emotional murmur.

"Some bastard put a cross in the casket! Block me so I can yank the damned thing out without anyone noticing. Open my bag!"

Thus my arthritic mother clumsily snatched a crucifix from her brother's wobbling casket with me as her human shield. Mom did the deed, kissed Bill goodbye, and we were back in our seats before the chanting procession reached the dais.

After the service, Neome slipped Perry an envelope with a letter that Bill had kept for more than six decades. It was from Mom's first husband, the one who fled soon after their son Timothy was born. This was how I learned that Mom had gone by the name Eleanor when she was a teenager.

July 21, 1946
2214 Nicholson St SE

Dear Bill,

Seeing as we are going to be related for a long time I thought it would be good to get acquainted, so I'll start the friendship off and hope that you follow it up.

Well Bill, we certainly wish you could have been here for the wedding, it was really very beautiful and I think we are both very lucky. You have Eleanor for a sister and I have her for a wife and boy I think she is really tops. I guess the best way to describe Eleanor is to just say she is the best little girl in town.

And another thing Bill, any worries that you have about Eleanor you can just forget about right now because I really love her with all my heart, and anything that happens to her will be over my dead body.

Although I have never seen you, I feel as though I have known you for a long time because Eleanor is always talking about you. And when I say that I want us to be good friends I really mean it.

Now Bill, you have our address so let us hear from you real soon. Let us know how you are getting along.

Well Bill, that's about all for now. Write soon.

Your Friend and Brother in Law,
Tennie.

P. S. It really broke Eleanor's heart when her mother didn't show up for the wedding.

As upsetting as this was to read, I appreciated finally knowing more of what Mom had gone through. Were her fragile emotions the result of these early relationship debacles—or did her jangled condition already exist and help put them into play? After Uncle

Bill was laid to rest, she and I had three hours to talk on the drive home to Portsmouth.

Mom told me that losing the two babies in her teens, as well as the support of her brother, was more than she could bear. She boarded a Greyhound bound for Vegas with plans to change her name—and then kill herself. Anonymously, so nobody would ever find out. After stepping off the bus amid the neon lights of the new city, Mom changed her name. But she also changed her mind.

"In the fifties Vegas was just starting and there were misfits like me from all over who showed up to create a new beginning. The atmosphere was so inspiring that instead of ending it all, I started fresh. Despite my lack of schooling, I was good with numbers and found work as a blackjack dealer. Eventually I carried on to Reno and dealt cards in a cowgirl outfit at Harold's Club. That's when I met your father, and you know the rest."

Chapter 13

A SWATH OF DIRT BECOMES A RIBBON OF ELEGANCE

"But I must gather knots of flowers, and buds and garlands gay,
For I'm to be Queen o' May, mother, I'm to be Queen o' May."
—British Poet Laureate Alfred, Lord Tennyson, Lincolnshire, 1833
—Me in our backyard, Portsmouth, 2009

Mother's Day was on the horizon. This meant that Mom and I nagged Jack to remember all three of his mothers. Perry, however, forbade us from celebrating with her. "Mother's Day is the most insincere Hallmark holiday—I don't participate in that bullshit. Take me out to lunch any other day of the year."

Her birthday, however, was always important.

With May upon us, I had six weeks to whip the house and yard into shape for Mom's eightieth birthday bash. After learning the grim details about her miserable youth, I was more determined than ever to make her golden years sparkle. This milestone birthday would have to be a showstopper.

It was already a warm spring, so we decided the gathering would be a garden party. This was a lofty goal, as our backyard was as derelict as "Grey Gardens," and Mom and I were as hapless as Big Edie and Little Edie, the film's zany mother-daughter duo.

I carefully pruned the scraggly rosebushes I had planted along the far fence, where they got the most sun. Mom hollered pointers from thirty feet away on the back deck, where she watched with binoculars. The unkempt yard was too uneven and dotted with weed mounds for her to totter across safely. I had tried and failed to seed the yard with grass, and could not afford the professional sodding proposed by a gardener.

Jack stopped by and joined me by the thorny rose shrubs.

"What you really need is a brick pathway from the deck to the back fence," he said. "It would allow Perry to walk to the roses and give the yard a total face-lift." Mr. Production Designer then pulled out his smartphone, looked up brick paths, and found an article on This Old House that showed "how to turn a swath of dirt into a ribbon of elegance in just one weekend."

"Sounds fantastic. But you know my back pops out if I crouch the wrong way pulling a sweater out of a drawer. If I attempted a brick path I'd end up more of an invalid than my mother."

"I didn't mean *you*," he laughed. "My series is dark next week and I'm off. I could do it then. Why don't we make it our birthday gift to your mom? Bricks are cheap. You cover that, and I'll do the installation. I did a paving job for a set once; it's monotonous but not difficult."

We hit Lowe's to find bricks that matched those in the path running along the side of the house. It would all blend perfectly. I was elated.

The next Monday morning, during the initial digging, Jack found a 1920s Portsmouth license plate, a relic still displayed on the mantel. As I left for work, our neighbor Fred shouted, "This is the kind of remodeling that will score you the lower mortgage I told you about!"

Jack was only half done when disaster struck. The archaic 1870 clay pipes that ran from the house to the sewer broke—flooding the side path with a torrent of our own turds. I was crestfallen. I rushed home to meet the plumber. He warned us not to use the toilets until the pipes were replaced.

"My guess is it'll cost you $2,400 for us to dig up the walkway, replace the broken pipes, level the path again, and re-lay the bricks."

"That's terrible," I grumbled, "but it doesn't seem like we have a choice."

"Your friend here looks like he knows what he's doing," the plumber observed. "If he wants to re-lay the side path after we fix the pipes, it would knock about a third off your bill."

Jack slowly stood up, appalled but pensive, with enough gravel dust on his shirtless torso to make him look like a sullen statue.

"I'm only off this week," Jack said with dread to the plumber. "When will you be finished fixing the pipes?"

"Tomorrow."

"As long as I have Thursday and Friday, I can do it."

When the plumber left, I went into the kitchen and explained the situation to Mom.

"Where do I go in the meanwhile?" she asked.

I pulled out our biggest, most scuffed-up pot and held it up.

"Danny, that's for soup."

"Now it's for poop."

Having to use the pot didn't bother Mom nearly as much as the idea of Jack having to stomp around in our caca doody. Before I headed back to the office, we anxiously brought him some iced tea.

"You don't have to go through with it," I said.

"I can try to get a higher limit on one of my cards," Mom offered.

"You both need to pay down your cards," Jack replied, taking a sip. Then he laughed. "I don't even *qualify* for a credit card now! What with the monthly support for my ex and her house with the kids . . ." He took another gulp. "Let's face it—all three of us are in deep shit. I don't mind doing my part to help dig us out. Anyway, I've had so many good dinners here—some of that muck is mine."

By the time Mom's eightieth birthday rolled around on June 11, the craggy backyard had magically transformed into a manicured garden.

While the centerpiece was Jack's perfectly aligned walkway, I added some oomph. Having given up on grass, I planted a bright, fast-growing ground cover with the wonderful name Creeping Jenny. My friend Eric came over with a few gallons of red stain for the weather-beaten back deck. Eric also brought a six-pack of Red Bull, which had us wielding rollers and brushes with the fervor of multi-armed dancing Hindu gods. That deck looked as good as new in no time.

My gardener friend David, who had helped me gauge Mom's drugs, drove down from DC a few days before the party to add finishing touches. In the back of his truck sat his heavy birthday gift for Perry: a stone bench carved like a cat. He and Jack lugged it to the end of the path so Mom had a place to sit and enjoy the pink Knockout roses, now in full bloom. David also pruned the trees and lined the back path with purple-flowered butterfly bushes, which made the newly verdant yard almost unrecognizable.

When Mom first stepped onto the brick walkway toward her bench, she had the same wide-eyed wonder that Dorothy did when she skipped down the Yellow Brick Road. Except Mom wasn't quite able to skip.

"After I die, *this* is where I'll make contact," Perry gleefully announced from the cat bench. "You boys have made this old broad happier than you can imagine."

The least likely home improvement was one Mom actually helped make herself. It was along the side path where the broken pipes had spewed our gunk over a month before. When I called David to bitch about the mishap, he reminded me that fresh excrement makes optimal fertilizer.

"Sprinkle morning glory and moonflower seeds in the little trench between the path and the house," he advised. "The mix of sun and shit should make them take off really fast."

Scattering seeds was one chore my unsteady mother could accomplish. I helped her do it along the base of the house as soon as Jack re-laid the bricks. Our dung had the effect of steroids. In just a few weeks, budding sprouts were climbing up the walls, obscuring ugly gas and drainage pipes. By mid-June, the vivid blue and white flowering vines reached the roof, making the fecal footpath look and smell like a botanical garden—even from the street.

"It's right out of *Jack and the Beanstalk*," Mom marveled.

I was beaming with pride the day my brothers Mike and Pat and their wives and kids flew in. As soon as they arrived in their overflowing rental car, we all took a leisurely evening stroll with Mom. We ambled alongside the mansions leading to High Street, where we turned and came upon a big birthday surprise: Mom's name up in lights on the grand marquee of the Commodore Theater:

HAPPY 80th PERRY LAWRENCE

Our neighbor Fred, who owns the theater, had just finished putting up the letters. He waved to us from the ladder, his pistol jangling in its belt holster. Despite her arthritis, Mom tossed her cane and posed with the agility of Jane Fonda at a premiere. My nephews, Mason and Grant, clicked away like paparazzi.

As the sun dropped in the warm blue sky, our garden party sizzled. Jack hung colored lanterns from the trees. Fred and Kas tended bar. Roderick played DJ. And Jenny set out a large eggless lemon cake with vanilla icing. David lit the candles and forty-odd friends from work, the Rainbow Cactus, and distant states joined in singing "Happy Birthday."

I wanted to make a good showing not just for Mom, but for Mike and Pat. My brothers had assumed most of the burden of looking after Mom in California for the previous decade. I wanted them to see that I could pull it together, too. Thankfully, they were visibly moved. Not just by the house and yard, but by our multigenerational circle of friends.

Mike's daughter, my seventeen-year-old niece, Paige, was sufficiently impressed that she announced she would leave LA for Norfolk to start college. This was wonderful news for me, and a major morale boost for Perry, who looked forward to some girl time with her granddaughter.

"You made it to eighty," I whispered to Mom as she wheezed onto the candles.

"*Almost,*" she huffed. "My lungs barely function; will you help me blow these damned things out?"

We blew the candles out together, and Mom opened presents, none of which I recall. All I remember is the gift I received a few days later.

The mortgage company sent an inspector to assess the property. The methodical assessor was charmed by the revamped interior—and blown away by the overhauled backyard. He declared the house was now worth $70,000 more than I had paid for it two years prior. This jump in value resulted in a new mortgage that reduced my monthly bill not by $500, as Fred had predicted, but a whopping $700.

The fixer-upper was finally fixed up. I no longer considered it a calamity; the house was now a home.

SUMMER 2010

Chapter 14

FLAGGED

The Fourth of July is a spectacle in Portsmouth, given the city's role as a naval hub during the Revolutionary War. Waking up to our third Independence Day in the house, I practically leapt out of bed giving a military salute as John Philip Sousa tunes echoed around the neighborhood.

In the little park across the street, an all-volunteer orchestra played marching anthems. Each performer brought a lawn chair and music stand, along with his or her tuba, clarinet, kettle drum, or xylophone. The conductor, who must have weighed four hundred pounds, brought a tiny, barely visible black stool as his perch. From behind, with his long, dark, stringy hair, he looked like a sumo wrestler stuck in a squat and waving a stick for help.

That year, because of the ninety-five-degree sticky heat, a smaller crowd than usual gathered in the park on scattered blankets, fanning themselves. Among them were me and Jack, pale Paige, and her husky, dusky boyfriend Geoffrey. He had long black dreads and piercing, starburst honey-colored eyes. At first I thought they were trendy contacts. It turned out he was born with pigmentation in the whites of his eyes, making it look like spiders had spun webs around his corneas. As if this weren't mesmerizing enough, he was a fiercely intelligent music major with off-the-cuff insights into whatever offbeat records we listened to upstairs. My mother liked him as much as I did, even though the low tone of his voice made him hard for her to understand. "I have no idea what he's saying but I hang on every word," she said.

We all tried to get Perry to join us for the lawn concert but she refused.

"My first love died fighting the Nazis—I do not wish to be reminded of 'bombs bursting in air,'" Mom said in the doorway as the band eked out a sloppy "Star-Spangled Banner." Humidity, patriotism, and especially flags made Perry crabby, and there was enough red, white, and blue bunting on our quaint street to cause her to convulse with conniption fits.

"Why do they hang these goddamned flags on their porches?" she bristled. "Are they afraid they're going to forget which country they live in?" Mom taught my brothers and me to be wary of patriotism, explaining, "It's delusional for every country to jump up and down and insist they are number one—that creates a pompous attitude toward other cultures and causes wars." Still, she *loved* the Olympics, always cheering loudest for underdog countries.

When we were kids, Mom taped to the refrigerator a quote by astronaut Frank Borman. It read, "When you're finally up by the moon, looking back at the earth, all these differences and nationalistic traits pretty well blend and you get a concept that maybe this is really one world and why the hell can't we learn to live together like decent people?"

That summer, the flag of Virginia flew from our porch—not so much out of pride, but because it featured the Roman goddess of virtue in a toga with her breast exposed. The design dates back to colonial times. Virginia has the only state flag featuring a bare boob, and our conservative attorney general had just made headlines for deriding its "lack of virtue." He even had new flag pins made with the barely visible tit covered up. Mom insisted we display the offending flag so that neighbors could see we were pro-nipple.

Well into our third year in the house, we had finally hit our stride. Since the golden reappraisal and refinancing the previous summer, I was no longer having monthly meltdowns when the mortgage was due. After ditching the stupefying opioids, Mom stopped having the bone-shattering falls—though she still swayed plenty. I encouraged her by telling her to think of herself as a Weeble, singing the TV jingle "Weebles wobble but they don't fall down."

Sadly, earlier that summer, Mom's old cat Sydney died. He had grown listless and stopped eating so I brought him to the vet, who diagnosed kidney failure. Daisy would die within a year from the same ailment. I don't know what traumas Sydney experienced before Mom adopted him. Like Daisy, he rarely came out from under her bed or left her side, except to use the litter box in the attached laundry room. Sydney did not like to be touched, and I didn't want him to feel uncomfortable in his last moments. When the vet was euthanizing him, rather than stroking his head, I got on my knees so that we could keep eye contact. I hoped he could see that he was loved despite his rough ride on this planet.

We lost Sydney but we gained Paige. A slender natural beauty with strong eyebrows and an easy smile, she roomed in Norfolk near Tidewater Community College, where she studied. I asked what she planned to major in.

"I have no idea. Like Nana, I just wanted to get the hell out of LA. I wanted to live on my own, and this was the only place my parents were okay with since you both are nearby."

Paige often rode her powder blue bike, basket full of books, aboard the Portsmouth ferry to join us for dinner, do homework, and listen to her crazy grandmother's off-color commentary during awards shows. She also brought a steady stream of college friends to our ever-expanding dinner parties. Paige instantly adapted to life in the Tidewater region, boasting on the phone to her father, "You can't get around by ferry and bike in LA."

Most significantly, after Jack and I had been together for more than a year, he vacated the apartment he was renting across the river and moved in with us. Though we became "a thing" the night we met, Jack and I continued to date others for a while. That arrangement lasted until we made the startling discovery that we were both having a fling with the same blond masseur. We had a laugh, and then decided it was time to upgrade our relationship from "friends plus" to boyfriends.

Now, at last, we were living in sin.

Having someone to share expenses, help look after Mom, and fix things around the house was a tremendous relief. But it was more than that. The three of us truly enjoyed spending time together. During late dinners, Mom shared her sarcastic take on that day's news, I gave updates on the latest laboratory PETA had busted, and Jack discussed set challenges for his series *A Haunting*. Many episodes involved ghoulish flashbacks to the 1890s, 1920s, or whatever year an evil spirit was said to have invaded the house in question. After dinner, Perry would scour the internet for photos of interiors from the decade Jack would be working on next, to help him with prep.

On weekends, we went thrift shopping. Jack hunted for period props, Mom perused books, and I hit records and housewares, always on the lookout for odd candleholders. We fluttered about like bowerbirds, the songbirds who constantly renovate their nests with colorful trash.   When we reconvened in the checkout line, Mom would examine my finds and invariably exclaim, "Not another goddamn sconce!"

Jack finally felt comfortable enough to introduce me to his family. He invited me to his daughter Asia's eighteenth birthday party at his ex-wife Anna's house in Norfolk. I say ex, but they had not yet formally filed for divorce. I urged him to get it over with, but Jack felt the dreaded process would be less upsetting for the whole family if he waited until Anna was seriously dating someone. From their exchanges, I knew Anna could be fiery, which made me anxious about our first meeting.

To my surprise, when she opened the door, she was practically beaming.

"Dan! Great to finally meet you!" she said with a hug.

Anna had olive skin, shoulder-length blonde hair with dark roots, a shapely figure, and a frisky smile. *It won't be long before she's re-hitched*, I thought. Awaiting us in the living room were Jack and Anna's teenage kids. Dylan was the oldest, followed by his sisters Mia, Asia, and Tess, the youngest. Each of them was as gracious to me as their mother was. No awkward moment, no ice to be broken. I felt instantly included in their clan. After witnessing their dad's torment as he grappled with coming out, they were simply happy that he was now happy. As we made our way to the dining room, a few of the birthday girl's young friends grinned approval when Asia introduced me as her dad's boyfriend. This made Jack misty-eyed. *Modern Family* had recently debuted on ABC and here we were living a real-life version.

"The tacos on that plate have Boca Burger Crumbles," said Anna as we took our seats. "I can't believe you turned Jack into a vegetarian—he was *totally* Mr. Ham and Cheese when we were together."

Jack had gone veggie? This was news to me. He had always politely ordered vegetarian at restaurants, and loved most of the grub we made at the house, but he never told me he had stopped eating meat altogether. I also never pushed him on it. My modus operandi with friends is not to be a nag, but a bitch in the kitchen, cooking up one delicious dish after another in hopes their taste buds would evolve. In Jack's case, he had also been exposed to a few gruesome slaughterhouse videos I edited at home after hours.

"When did you go veg?" I whispered.

"Oh, I guess a few months ago. It happened gradually; there was no big moment. They bring in catering at the studio; they always have a veggie option and I found myself just getting that. I didn't want to make a big deal about it in case it didn't stick. But it did. Surprise! I told Anna and the kids so they knew to have something other than meat. Anna was always the healthier eater anyway."

After Asia's birthday bash, Jack and I arrived home to find Perry having a surprising family moment of her own. She had decided not to join us for the party as she worried it would be impossible for her to read people's lips or distinguish voices in such a large group. However, she had no problem distinguishing the voice on the phone—whoever it was—as she gabbed away in the kitchen. Walking through the front door, Jack and I were intrigued by the animated conversation, so we quietly eavesdropped from the foyer.

"When is the last time she even heard well enough to carry on a phone conversation?" Jack whispered.

"I don't know, years. Maybe she ordered a new one online with supersonic earbuds."

"You really *must* see this movie," Mom exclaimed. "Your grandfather is from Russia, though he left when he was younger than you are now. What's that? Oh, I think he was about six. They fled the anti-Jewish pogroms at the turn of the century. Look it up. Anyway, you are part Russian and this film really shows the soul of the country. Grab a pen and write it down."

Mom paused for several seconds.

"She must be talking to one of my nephews, or to Paige," I whispered. "My dad's dad fled Russia as a child."

"All set? It's called *Moscow Does Not Believe in Tears.*" She relayed the title slowly so that the person she was talking to could write it down. "Got it? It won an Oscar back in '81, though I know that's way before your time, Grant." Grant was my teenage nephew in Los Angeles.

"I'd send you my VHS but you probably don't have a player," she continued. "Watch it on Netflix, or watch when you visit again."

I started to feel guilty snooping, so we walked into the kitchen.

"Hi, Mom," I said casually.

"Oh, hi, Danny, I was just catching up with Grant, he sounds great." She was all smiles but held no phone in her hand. Jack and I subtly scoured the kitchen island she was leaning against and spotted no phone there, either.

It was another imaginary conversation.

At first, I was startled. Was this glitch from the same part of Mom's aging brain that made her think she heard a plane crash, ghosts of children playing on the stairs, and off-key big-band numbers? Then I thought about what a comparatively pleasant "exchange" it was—she had even spoken fondly about my dad's side of the family, which was often a bitter subject.

Old people can get stuck in recall mode. I figured it must be soothing for Mom to conjure up such a nice blend of memories over a fake phone, especially in the safe environment of our home, where I could monitor such delusions. When I moved her in, I had no idea Mom would be bringing along so many imaginary friends, but this was all part of my fluid responsibility as her guardian.

As long as the fantasy discussions remain positive, where's the harm?

Chapter 15

GADABOUTS

With Mom puttering along, Jack around, and Paige nearby, I was able to resume my nomadic do-gooding beyond the occasional overnight jaunt.

One week I crisscrossed the country wearing a suit and toting a bull hook, which is like a fireplace poker but sharper. Circus trainers use them to beat elephants backstage, inflicting wounds they then have to camouflage from the public with gray spray paint. I showed the cruel instrument to reporters in cities where Ringling Bros. was set to perform, which resulted in decent editorials in the *Dallas Morning News* and *Boston Globe*.

Flying on to New York, I plopped my carry-on onto the X-ray belt and instantly realized I'd forgotten to pack the steel-tipped club in my checked bag. Naturally, the alarm went off and the

TSA guard hollered that he had to go through my bag. I was furious with myself; these bull hooks were hard to obtain. What if it was confiscated? Shockingly, when the guard inspected my bag, he overlooked the concealed weapon and only pulled out a bottle of water. I was lucky. In New York, I was set to appear on the *Today* show to display and describe the device to a national audience. With no bull hook to wave around, I would have had to play an awkward game of charades. When the segment aired, Mom texted her congratulations before I had even left the set.

My last stop was Bridgeport, Connecticut, hometown of circus founder P. T. Barnum. There the *Connecticut Post* ran a front-page story headlined "Armed with a 'Smoking Gun', PETA Takes Fresh Aim at the Use of Circus Elephants" and an editorial declaring, "The animals have got to go." (After six more years of protests, that's just what happened: first, Ringling pulled the elephants and then the circus closed for good in 2017, after 146 years.)

With Jack at home looking after Perry, I was also able to reengage with the gay rights crusade. I gleefully accepted an invitation to Knoxville, Tennessee, to help train activists from across the country to disrupt Obama events. The goal was to pressure the president to make good on his pledge to repeal "Don't Ask, Don't Tell."

A few years into his administration, Obama had not made a move to fulfill this promise but continued to benefit from millions raised from gay donors. One such donor, Jonathan Lewis, was so infuriated that he flew activists to the Highlander Center in Tennessee to make battle plans. He aimed to use his access to get stealthy protestors into Obama fund-raisers to heckle the president to keep his word. As I had made a career of weaseling my way past security guards to disrupt fur fashion shows, my friend Paul Yandura, whose group GetEqual organized the summit, asked me to be among the speakers.

"Secret Service agents scan the crowd for people who look uncomfortable," I told the hundred or so budding militants. "It's nerve-racking to agitate like this, especially against someone most of us voted for, but you've got to relax, smile, and make small talk before he takes the stage. Otherwise they'll spot you and kick you out."

I was surprised to meet a police officer among the rabble-rousers; she was a spunky butch blonde with whom I kept in touch for a while. The infiltration plans soon went into effect in New York, LA, and Miami, repeatedly embarrassing the president on the evening news. Within a few months, he fast-tracked the repeal, announcing, "No longer will tens of thousands of Americans in uniform be asked to live a lie, or look over their shoulder."

Mom was so proud she emailed me a slew of articles about the historic change in Pentagon policy. The outpouring of public support for Obama when he repealed "Don't Ask, Don't Tell" laid the groundwork for the president to change his position and support marriage equality. Landmark gay rights achievements ended up among Obama's most lasting legacies, but, as with all social issues, it didn't happen without some push and shove.

———

My mother, who by now realized she was too frail to be a fire-brand on the streets as she once was, radiated pride every time I took off for an activist junket. She never once got irritable when I was away, in part because she had developed such a lively social life through our various friends. If Jack and Paige were busy, many others stepped in to look after her.

Jenny from PETA often took Perry to dinner at Olive Garden. From a high-top table in the bar area, the pair would eat salad and bruschetta while exchanging snarky observations about other diners' hairstyles or ill-fitting pantsuits. They wrote their comments on paper place mats. Once, a serene white-haired woman walked by and cooed to Jenny about my innocent-looking mother: "*Awww*, isn't she a sweet lady?"

"If you only knew!" Jenny replied, quickly moving her glass of iced tea to cover a vulgar comment Perry had just scrawled about that very woman. The refined matron had been fanning herself vigorously in the waiting area, about which Mom wrote, "It looks like she's jacking off."

If Mom needed a lift during the day, my dimpled, tattooed friend Riley pitched in, since he worked nights as a DJ in a strip club. Riley drove her to the library, the eye doctor, or cemeteries. Perry was a volunteer for Find-A-Grave, a site on which far-flung friends or relatives search for locals to put flowers on the grave of a long-lost loved one. Portsmouth, being such an old town, boasts beaucoup dead people going back to the 1600s, many of them buried in fancy, decaying tombs at Cedar Grove Cemetery near our house.

"We look sooo *Harold and Maude*," Perry told young Riley,

hanging on to his bicep as they traipsed over graves, looking for a barely legible headstone on which to lay orchids.

Mom's best late-night friend was Doc Holliday's boyfriend John, who was a vice principal at a special needs high school. He had the rare gift of speaking in a tone that Perry could actually hear. This was handy as they had a lot to talk about, especially politics. John appreciated an after-dinner drink. He often visited Mom with his bawdy navy nurse friend, Amy, who liked to blow off steam between deployments to the Middle East. They occasionally took Perry to one of the noisy honky-tonk bars near the shipyard. Other times, they came over to hang out on the couch and watch the latest indie film Mom had received in a red envelope from Netflix.

If I was out of town working, Mom often teased me by texting a photo of her with some gadabout from our circle of friends. "We're at Baron's Pub and you're not!" These messages made me euphoric. They were little scraps of evidence that I had made the right decision in moving her in. In one text, Mom claimed she was having as much fun at eighty-one as she'd had at twenty-one. Now that I knew more about the tragic heartbreaks she endured at that earlier age, I almost believed her.

Chapter 16

TWAIN OF THOUGHT

As well as things were going at home, Jack and I were both itching for a break from family responsibilities.

Finally, that summer, he was able to join me for a waterside weekend work trip. It was our first getaway and we were ecstatic, even if our destination was not glamorous Key West or Province-town, but Hannibal, Missouri, a dusty village on the muddy Mississippi River. From what I had read, the city was much like Portsmouth: a historic port town well past its prime, brimming with magnificent old mansions and aimless young addicts.

Built in 1871 (just a year after our house), the Robards Man-sion in Hannibal was a two-story redbrick Victorian converted into a bed-and-breakfast. When we schlepped our bags from the white-columned porch into the ornate foyer, it felt like a Gilded

Age home away from home. That is, until the cranky couple who ran the place saw that our party of two sharing one bed consisted of two dudes.

"You sure you don't want a room with two beds?" the white-haired man grumbled.

"We'll stick with the one we reserved, please," I replied. "The parlor room with the four-poster bed." I winked at Jack. Unaccustomed to homophobic encounters, he smiled uneasily.

Our grizzled host reluctantly gave me the key, pointed to the carpeted flying staircase, and shook his head as he rejoined his wife in the kitchen. So much for southern hospitality. I'm glad we stuck by our guns. Our room had tall ceilings, nine-foot windows, a marble fireplace, blue patterned wallpaper, and Victorian curio cabinets packed with creepy ceramic figurines. Jack unpacked while I read aloud from the B&B's brochure.

"It says 'your hosts will do everything possible to make your stay pleasant.' Jack, why don't you go down and tell them we forgot condoms and lube and see if they have any on hand."

Jack laughed and then tackled me onto the four-poster bed. He pinned me down, kissed me, and stretched my hands to the far corners of the patchwork quilt. With a devilish grin, he said, "I think these four posts might come in handy."

We were in Hannibal for the unveiling of an exhibit at Mark Twain's Boyhood Home & Museum, chronicling the author's maverick animal rights views. I'm no fiction aficionado, but I had admired Twain's blunt essays when I read them in a high school lit class. His animal rants were unknown to the average *Tom Saw-*

yer fan, so I proposed a PETA-sponsored display as one of the special events marking the centennial of his death. The museum director, always on the lookout for new ways to attract visitors, loved the idea. I compiled passages, quotes, and photos for the museum to produce on panels, and then flew in to speak at a press reception. I was more excited going to Hannibal than I would have been going to Hawaii.

Strolling around the tree-lined streets of "America's Hometown," Jack and I noticed Old Glory waving from just about every elegant Victorian. I wondered if residents knew their hometown hero's views on patriotism. They matched those of my mother. Twain wrote: "Man is the only Patriot. He sets himself apart in his own country, under his own flag, and sneers at the other nations."

As we walked past the elegant stone First Christian Church, I thought of Twain's take on faith: "Man is the only Religious Animal. He is the only animal that has the True Religion—several of them. He is the only animal that loves his neighbor as himself, and cuts his throat if his theology isn't straight."

Twain's passion for animals came about exactly as mine would more than a century later: his mother took in stray cats. (She also confronted men who beat their horses on the mean streets of Missouri before the Civil War.) Twain became obsessed with cats, his daughter Susy once commenting, "The difference between Papa and Mama is Mama loves morals and Papa loves cats." Twain could not pass a cat on the street without stopping to say hello—something I do, too. Inspired by Darwin, he observed animals wherever he traveled, but what set Twain apart was his chronicling of their distinct personalities, whether he was writing about a mutt, a robin, a camel, or a frog.

Animals were central in many of Twain's stories. Huck Finn was reduced to sobs studying the limp body of a songbird he shot, swearing he would never again kill another creature. Twain's tirades against hunting went very much against the grain in Missouri, then and now. I wondered how locals would respond to my talk at the museum.

In his later years, Twain wrote a pamphlet against animal experiments: "I am not interested to know whether Vivisection produces results that are profitable to the human race or doesn't," because of "the pains which it inflicts upon unconsenting animals."

Under a warm blue sky, the Saturday afternoon launch event at Twain's rustic home drew about fifty enthusiastic locals. Many brought their dogs, whose barks punctuated the little speech I gave. After unveiling the exhibit with the museum director, we took questions. A woman wearing shorts and big glasses raised her hand and asked if Twain's animal advocacy had any lasting impact.

"Yes—in a surprising way," I replied. "One artist he inspired was fellow Missourian Walt Disney, who produced the first live-action nature movies starting in the 1940s. Like Twain, he focused on the playful personalities of animals, a big contrast to contemporaries like Ernest Hemingway and Teddy Roosevelt, who bragged about how many animals they killed and posed with their carcasses. The Disney documentaries won Oscars and influenced future generations when they aired on TV in the sixties and seventies. Also, like Twain did in his stories, Disney sided with fictional animals on issues like hunting in *Bambi* and elephants in the circus in *Dumbo*."

As the event wound down, the *Hannibal Courier-Post* snapped a photo of me signing the white picket fence around Twain's home, modeled on the fence whitewashed in *Tom Sawyer*. I scribbled a shout-out to Twain, his mother, Jane, and their cats in Hannibal, from me, my mother, Perry, and our cats in Portsmouth.

Jack snapped a picture, too, and texted it to my mom and Paige, who had stayed over with her the Saturday we were away. Mom was delighted with our occasional updates and always looked forward to whatever trinket we brought home for her.

After a celebratory dinner with the museum staff, Jack and I were longing to experience modern-day, gritty Hannibal, away from the tourists.

"If you want the real deal, go to the Down Under Lounge," advised Cindy, the museum director. "But don't say I didn't warn ya!"

Tucked beneath the 1888 Federal Building, the Down Under was a smoky, subterranean labyrinth of wooden halls lined with bar stools, chipped stone pillars, and a low, faded copper ceiling. The only light came from dim wall lamps, the glow of an old cigarette machine, and a jukebox blasting the All-American Rejects. A small, busy bar was wedged into an exposed brick archway at the far end. *Heaven on Earth*, we thought. At least under it.

Jack and I waited in line to order beers and observed the loud, rowdy, mixed-age crowd. Two guys with tattoos embroidered on their faces downed shots while hollering at each other and nearly slipping off their bar stools. Other boisterous conversations echoed throughout the basement bar under a hazy layer of smoke. It was Saturday night in a Wild West saloon where a fistfight could break out at any moment. As dive bar enthusiasts, we loved the place, but Jack and I were clearly "not from around these parts." I wondered if this bunch had the same attitude toward gays as our ill-mannered innkeeper.

"Look, but don't make eye contact," I said to Jack with a laugh. We had barely sipped our PBRs when a striking, dark-haired young man in black approached us.

"Where are you guys from?" He smiled. He had wide, friendly eyes and exuded confidence but not aggression.

"Virginia," Jack replied.

"Well, welcome to Hannibal! It's good to see people like you here."

"People like us?" We were yelling in order to hear each other above the din of drunken chatter and clanging guitars. The friendly local rested a hand on each of our shoulders and pulled in for a huddle.

"There's not really a gay scene here," he said. "We're way behind the times."

"Are we that obvious?" Jack asked.

"You stood out to me. Most of this crowd is probably too hammered to notice. It's a good thing you're not holding hands though, especially around here."

"Right," I replied. "We realized that when we checked into our B&B and they wanted to separate us into two beds."

"I'm not surprised. I'm Travis, by the way." We introduced ourselves and clicked cans.

"Missouri has the distinction of being the first state to ban gay marriage a few years back," he reminded us. "Half a million more people than usual went to the polls just to vote for it. It passed with such an angry mob mentality that many gay people, especially in small towns, prefer to fly below the radar. I'm not out myself—not even to my bandmates!"

"You're in a band?" I said. "We were looking for live music earlier but couldn't find anything."

"Come see *us*! We're playing in a warehouse at the edge of town in about an hour. I'll give you the address—but don't say anything about what I just told you."

Was this the beginning of a true crime reality show, at the end of which Jack and I would be found dead in a cornfield? Nah, Travis was a total pussycat—or a skilled sociopath.

We followed the directions scribbled on the napkin, driving outside city limits along dark country lanes to a desolate, rural intersection. I couldn't imagine a band playing anywhere near here. Soon we came upon a dirt lot full of cars. We parked and followed a swarm of smokers in hoodies to a large brick ware-house pulsing with music. The band had just started a set of melodic indie metal. Our new friend was the guitarist, and when they finished he waved us to the side of the small stage.

"Glad you guys made it." Travis introduced us to the band as they unplugged their amps. He reached into a cooler and handed us each a beer.

"Impressive set," I said. "You into Silversun Pickups? We've been listening to *Swoon* nonstop and just saw them in Norfolk."

"I haven't heard the new one but I love 'Lazy Eye' from their last album. I wanted to see them in St. Louis but didn't make it."

"At least there seems to be an okay music scene here in Hannibal," Jack added, glancing around at the sociable audience.

"'Okay' is accurate. Summer is fun here. Anyway, the night is young! Our friend Becky is having a bonfire at her farm out on Route Z at midnight. Why don't you guys join us?"

As we were in Hannibal, I instantly pictured Becky Thatcher from *The Adventures of Tom Sawyer*. Would she be welcoming this scruffy bunch in a white summer frock and embroidered pantalettes, her yellow hair plaited into two long tails?

Not exactly. When we stepped onto the porch of her pastoral farmhouse, we found Becky to be more of a plain Jane, in ripped jeans and a sweatshirt, but she was every bit as courteous as Miss Thatcher.

"We're friends of Travis," Jack said.

"Welcome! Beer's in the kitchen, fire's out back," Becky chirped with a southern drawl.

"Thanks," I said. "By the way, what kind of farm is this? It's hard to tell in the dark." I was worried we might walk out back and find a shed crammed with doomed chickens or pigs.

"Oh, we just have a little apple orchard. You can make out the treetops over there. We also have pet goats out back and they are very friendly, especially if you feed them carrots or hay—that's in the barn, help yourself!"

We galloped straight to the goats, who looked like wizards

with their beards and horns. There were half a dozen in a large pen, though only a few were interested in eating at that hour. I got on the ground, reclined against a post, and got into a staring contest with a spellbinding brown and white billy goat. He won.

Jack pitched in to help build the bonfire. There wasn't enough dry wood to create the sort of inferno a pyro like me appreciates, but the subdued, witching-hour flames made the stars overhead sparkle even brighter in the indigo sky. Travis arrived with the band, lugging his guitar so he could strum songs for the fifteen or so friends surrounding the fire.

We recognized several of the rowdy individuals from the Down Under Lounge. In this serene setting, where the cigarette smoke was replaced with burning cinder and pot fumes, they were more peaceful and reflective. The chilly night air prompted a few couples to cuddle. Jack and I did the same—and our affection drew a few apprehensive stares. Travis tried not to notice as he played "Black Hole Sun," which kept everyone rapt for a few minutes. Finally, someone spoke.

"I'm sorry people are so unfair to y'all," said a twentysomething blonde across the smoky pit, her eyes made up like a raccoon's. Her skinhead boyfriend looked away from us into the distance for a beat, and then vaguely nodded in agreement.

"That's very kind, thanks," I replied, squeezing Jack's hand. "You get used to it. When I was in junior high, they tried to ban gays from working in schools throughout California. The bill almost passed and created all kinds of hostility. I got beaten up between classes, felt like an outlaw at thirteen, and don't feel much different now. I was lucky because my mom helped me fight to get the bullies suspended. When the vice principal made excuses for them she ripped him a new one, right in front of the little bastards and their parents."

"She sounds like a badass," said the band's long-haired singer.

"You have no idea," Jack said, laughing. "We all live together now and she's just as outspoken."

Travis said nothing; he just kept playing his guitar and grinning as one nice comment after another seeped out of his friends. Not everyone was supportive. Some of the young men were conspicuously silent and looked annoyed as they took drags off their cigarettes.

"You know what's funny," Jack said, looking at them. "Many of those belligerent guys from high school found Dan on Facebook. They wrote that they were sorry for just going along with the crowd and being mean. It was just a stupid phase. He was glad to hear from them and kept in contact. It shows people can rise above."

Travis looked over at us, smiled, and nodded.

"Well, it's getting late," I said. "I don't think the old sourpuss at our B&B would be keen on a couple of homos asking for late checkout on the Lord's Day. Thanks for having us!"

"Good to meet y'all," said Becky. "If you ever get back to Hannibal let's hang out again!" Several of our new friends hugged us goodbye, and Travis walked us to the car.

"Thanks, guys. This ended up being a great night."

"Thanks for including us," said Jack. "And you should come out to your friends. I found it a lot easier than I imagined; you'd be surprised."

"It was a relief to hear a few of them say what they did, but I'm not so sure I want to do that yet."

"They probably already know, especially after you had us along tonight!" I said. "I bet one of them has a crush on you. Could be the one who is most antagonistic. Maybe this time next year you'll be living together."

Our first trip together had developed into quite the outing. Jack and I felt like the leads in *Route 66*, the old series in which two road trippers drive into a town as strangers and end up embedded in local, personal intrigue. They made new friends in each episode before splitting to the next town. Jack and I would follow this pattern on nearly all of our future trips, and, oddly, the adventures often involved musicians.

The next morning we checked out bleary-eyed. Our host was every bit as cold as he was when we checked in. He didn't even speak until I plopped the key onto the desk. Then he growled like a sick buzzard.

"When you leave here I suggest you two take yourselves straight to church! Living like you do—you've got some prayin' to do."

Having barely wiped the sleep from our eyes, we were shocked at the outburst. I lost control.

"Sounds like you feel guilty, having personally profited from renting your room to homosexuals. But I've got to thank you— your obsession with our sex lives ended up being quite a turn-on. The bed frame was a little squeaky but your mattress was very comfortable; we'll recommend this place to all of our friends."

The geezer huffed and his lips curled but he didn't say anything more. He just turned around, quivering with anger, and once again joined his silent wife in the kitchen.

"I'm sorry," I told Jack as we walked to the car. "Every once in a while you just snap, you know?"

"I've never seen you like that!" He laughed. We packed up the trunk and got into our little rented Honda.

"Oh shit!" screamed Jack.

"Don't tell me you forgot your wallet or something and we have to go back in there."

"I forgot to take the curtain ties off the bedposts! That poor guy's imagination is really going to go wild now."

Chapter 17

PREMATURE BURIAL

We arrived in Portsmouth still aglow from Becky's bonfire. Walking through the door, we found a much eerier fire ceremony.

Mom had the lights out and candles blazing all around the living room and kitchen. She lit candles only when someone died. The deceased didn't need to be a friend or relative: it could be a pro golfer she once had the hots for or a bus driver swept into a flood on the Weather Channel.

Jack and I walked to Perry's room and found her sitting on her bed next to Daisy. Daisy was on her last legs, but she used her paws to massage Mom's thighs. Mom had a detached look on her face. Whoever had died must have been someone she knew—or Alex Trebek. Jack brought our bags upstairs and I called Paige, who had spent the night before with Mom at the house.

"Nana was normal last night," Paige reported. "Well, she's never normal but you know what I mean."

I went in to gently ask Mom who had croaked. Having been through this ritual since childhood, I simply took a seat on the bed and clasped her hand.

"The candles are for Helen," she sniveled without looking at me.

Helen was a kooky friend of Mom's from New York who wore the same exact cat-eye glasses since the fifties. They hadn't seen each other in years.

"I'm so sorry. How did it happen? I didn't know Helen was ill."

"No idea, I only just found out. May she rest in peace."

"Can I get you some water?"

"That would be nice, thanks."

Mom trudged behind me into the kitchen, where the shadowy gold-hued walls flickered with candlelight. I turned on a hanging lamp and grabbed a few glasses. Glancing to the stove, I noticed one candle burning particularly brightly. It was just a white taper candle, but it had been stuck into a vase full of coffee beans. The oily beans had started to ignite.

"Mom, coffee beans are flammable; this is very dangerous." I spoke plainly, not in a scolding manner. I felt bad about her friend dying.

"Oh, I had no idea; sorry, Danny. I'm just so upset."

As I poured the water, I started to wonder more about Helen.

"Who told you about Helen dying?" I asked. "I can't think of who your mutual friends are."

"I don't know. Somebody just told me, that's all."

"Who is 'somebody'?"

"What difference does it make?"

That's when it hit me. I bet another mystery voice had engaged Mom in an imaginary conversation—only this time it was not good-natured. I walked back into her bedroom, found her cell, and dialed Helen. After just a few rings, she answered in her exuberant Brooklyn accent.

"Hi, Helen, how are you? It's Danny calling on Perry's phone."

"I'm doing fine! Wonderful to hear from you! How's your mom?"

"She's okay, she's right here, I'll put her on." I walked back into the kitchen and tried to hand the phone to my mother. "It's Helen. She sounds great and she's at home. Why don't you say hello."

My mother looked at me with a combination of shock and anger.

"I don't believe you," she hissed softly, in an apparent attempt to keep dead Helen from overhearing. I covered the receiver.

"Just say hi and try to hear her voice for a second."

Mom refused and plodded back into her bedroom, where she sat and stroked her cat and stared into space.

"I'm sorry, Helen, we'll have to call you back later, she's got her hands full in the kitchen, but it meant a lot to me to hear your voice. Please visit when you can!" I hung up and went upstairs to give Jack the lowdown. In hopes of easing her out of her spooky mood, he brought down the jar of apricot jam we had picked up for her on our trip.

———

The Helen saga passed, but Mom remained withdrawn. She lost interest in what Jack and I were working on, opted out of joining us to eat in the dining room, and winced at the suggestion of leaving the house for a last-minute movie or a bite, as she once loved to do. Now she rarely left her room or changed out of her nightgown.

On a bright Saturday morning, Jack and I walked downstairs to find Mom in her robe busily stacking all of her clothes and books in the foyer and den. "Spring cleaning feels good any time of year, doesn't it?" I said with a kiss. She barely looked at me. Like an automaton, she just kept adding to the stacks.

"The guy from Goodwill is coming at noon," she muttered. "I want everything to be neat for him to cart away." I started to quiz her about it but bit my tongue. Jack played along too and simply poured her a cup of coffee, no questions asked. Mom's mess cluttered up the living room and entryway for several days, until another voice must have told her to put everything back. Watching TV among her piles of debris for a week was a small price to pay for peace.

One night, Paige came over to set up a Skype between Mom and her old friend Molly in California. Molly and Perry were brassy bookkeepers at a dull law firm together in the sixties. A few nights a week after work, they drank margaritas, danced to a mariachi band, flirted with the string section, and shared laughs before going home to their fledgling families. Half a century later, Molly had Alzheimer's and could barely speak and Perry only seemed to hear make-believe voices; Molly's son Greg called me to arrange for them to see each other one last time via Skype.

Ten minutes before the call, Mom muttered, "I don't think I can go through with this."

Paige tried to reassure her: "It's easy. I'll hold up the phone, you'll see Molly, she'll see you, just say what you want."

"Oh, I don't know."

"Mom, you have to do this," I insisted. "It'll take ten minutes and will make Molly very happy, plus her kids and grandkids will be there. They've got her all made up in her hospice bed."

"She's probably so out of it she won't even recognize me. Plus I look like shit."

I may not have been able to get Mom out of the house, but I was determined for her to reconnect with her old friend on Skype. It could only do her good. Perry needed to have an exchange with an actual living, breathing friend—even if Molly was barely there at that point. As she continued making excuses, an idea came to mind. I dashed upstairs to a trunk in which we kept Halloween garb. I found a gray granny wig and pulled it on as I ran back downstairs a few minutes before the call. I looked like Anthony Perkins at the end of *Psycho*.

"Mom, if you don't do the call with Molly, I'll impersonate you and do it myself. Which story about you and Molly's carousing shall I share first? I bet her grandkids have no idea what she was like before she became born again."

"All right! All right!" Mom laughed. "I'll do the fucking Skype—but five minutes max. And you do it with me so I don't look like a total imbecile when I can't understand what they're saying."

Poor Molly did not utter a word; she just grinned while her

extended Mexican-American family surrounded her and did most of the talking. Mom sprang to life, however. She introduced Paige to Molly's grandkids and recalled the time she and Molly joined Cesar Chavez's march for migrant farmworkers. As Perry had been so despondent lately, it was nice to see her old spark resurface.

After the call, pumped up from the excitement, Mom happily sat down with us for a chatty Chinese dinner.

It would be our last carefree evening together for a very long time.

Chapter 18

FLAMEOUT

I should have hidden the candles.

That was my first thought when I walked in after work. It had been a hot, breezy August day, the kind you hate to spend cooped up in an office. I had considered joining friends for a Virginia Beach cookout but instead I went home to check on Mom— a previously routine chore that now filled me with dread. Once again, I found candles blazing around the darkened downstairs. When I plopped my laptop bag onto the kitchen island, Mom rushed out to see me. She was panic-stricken.

"Danny, you've got to hurry back out the door to the airport and fly to LA. Your father has had a stroke—he's dying and doesn't have much time left. *Hurry!*"

"I haven't heard anything about it." I tried to appear both

concerned and unruffled. "Let me call Mike and Pat and check it out."

"Don't bother Mike! He's still in the hospital recovering from that heart attack."

I called my brothers. Mike had not had a heart attack, and aside from bouts of forgetfulness, our father was fine. Mom's once-innocuous daydreams had morphed into wide-awake nightmares. I told my brothers about the previous episode involving Helen, as well as about Mom's recurring candle fetish.

"The fantasy conversations have been going on for a long time but her mood has darkened," I said. "Doc Holliday and I have tried to get Mom to see a neurologist but she refuses to even discuss it. She'll only go to the eye doctor, the dentist, and the geriatric specialist to get her heart and lung meds renewed. That's Dr. Harrison; he keeps an eye on her COPD. She's fond of him at least, and the next appointment is coming up soon."

"If she trusts him, bring it up when you're all together so she has to deal with it," said Pat. "It sounds awful. If you need our help just say the word and one of us will be on the next flight out."

"I will, and that day is coming soon. Let's hope the doctor offers some insight in a few weeks."

"Meanwhile," said Mike, "I'll email her a picture of us with Dad from last weekend—maybe that will convince her we're not in intensive care."

Those few weeks were difficult to get through. Perry continued fuming that I had fact-checked Helen's death, Dad's stroke, and Mike's heart attack. Our relationship became strained and antagonistic. Any attempt I made to be social prompted an outburst of rage, which caused me to retreat upstairs. Working for an organization that exposes graphic cruelty to animals, I had come to cherish evenings at home as an escape from the harsh world. Now I faced more tension at home than I did in the office and it was wearing me down.

One night, shortly after my twenty-fifth anniversary at PETA and a promotion to senior vice president, I slogged home and found Mom sitting in the dark gazing at her computer. The blue light of the monitor illuminated the downcast expression on her face. When she saw me, she slowly turned her head toward me and growled.

"I heard you got fired! We're going to end up homeless! Is that what you want?"

Another evening I found a note from Mom on the kitchen island: "Please remove the Virginia flag—the exposed breast really is pornographic and it's embarrassing." I wondered what caused her to change her mind. Was she now hearing the voice of Pat Robertson? I didn't dare ask. I just took the flag down.

Not long after, Jack and I were sprawled on the couch watching *American Horror Story*. Mom spookily appeared between the red and gold curtains dividing the living room and the kitchen. We had drawn them together to prevent another arbitrary provocation. Looking like a disheveled witch, Mom pointed dramatically to the red swag lamp in the front window, where it had been hanging for years.

"That red light signals to everyone that this is a whorehouse!"

We laughed at first. It was just like the random sort of joke Mom used to make. Unfortunately, she was not kidding—nor was she finished.

"You guys cannot lay together on the couch like that," she raged. "People are gathering on the street outside and staring. What must they be thinking? It's just not right, Danny, I have to live here, too!" It was hard to believe this was Mom talking. Only a year before, when a little old lady in an elevator said to me, "You're so tall you must have to get on your knees to kiss the girls!" Mom quipped, "He's gay; he gets on his knees all right but it's not to kiss the girls."

I sprang off the couch to the front window. I looked through the gauzy drapes. There wasn't a soul on the veranda or on the street. Even if there had been passersby, they could not have seen into the living room without climbing over the porch railing and peering through the curtains. Rather than argue, we retreated upstairs. More than aggravated, Jack and I were sad and perplexed. Mom was not only helplessly miserable, but she was lashing out in attempts to involve us in her mania. Our funhouse had turned into a madhouse.

Finally, the morning of the appointment with Dr. Harrison arrived.

I had not reminded Mom of the visit the day before for fear of her conjuring some excuse to squirm out of it. An hour before we had to leave, I simply gave her a friendly reminder about the prescriptions she needed to bring in for him to refill. To sweeten the deal in case she balked, I suggested we stop by the library afterward, where Perry liked to check out the latest spy novels and bird-watching books. That idea perked her up. For the first time in weeks, she actually smiled, which almost made me cry. I was extremely relieved when Mom started putting on clothes to leave the house.

Dr. Harrison was a tall, sturdy army veteran. He was friendly, patient, and clear without being condescending, valuable virtues for anyone treating seniors—especially my mother. Luckily, Perry had a crush on him and was less argumentative than she had been with other physicians.

Due to her near deafness, Mom had me accompany her during any exam so that she was clear on whatever the doctor said. This had been our routine since she moved in. Sometimes it became a comedy routine. Once, when she had a painful digestive attack, an ER doctor mumbled that he had to give her a rectal exam. Perry could not understand him, despite his repeated, hilarious attempts to word the request in different ways. Finally, I had to yell, *"He needs to stick his finger up your ass!"* Without missing a beat, Mom hollered to him, "Have at it but it's been years since anyone touched me there." Laughter erupted throughout the emergency room. I was sad to think that such Hallmark moments might now be done.

Mom forced a weary smile when Dr. Harrison checked her heartbeat, looked into her ears, and gauged her breathing. I was nervous and fidgety. When would be the right moment to bring up the frightful incidents that showed she was losing her grip on reality?

Finally, Dr. Harrison was finished with the checkup. He looked at both of us and asked, "Is there anything else going on, anything out of the ordinary I should know about?"

"Nope," said Mom instantly. She quickly began putting on her coat. "Everything's just fine, thank you."

"Actually, there has been an escalating problem," I said. Mom stiffened. Her smile faded.

"What's that?" asked Harrison.

"She keeps thinking people are dying or having strokes or heart attacks. Like my brother and father and her friend. But none of this actually happened and she gets angry when I call and find out they're all right."

Mom was bristling. It was as if we were high school students in the principal's office and I had just snitched on her for vandalizing the gym.

"Tell me about this, Perry."

"Don't listen to him."

He leaned in. "It's okay to talk about it."

"There's nothing to talk about! Jesus Christ, what is wrong with you people?" Tears suddenly began streaming from her eyes. Mom squirmed down from the exam table and stormed out of the office, slamming the door behind her.

"Dr. Harrison, I don't know what to do," I said, trembling. "My mother has become so full of delusional rage that it's hard to be around her. She won't see anyone else. Bringing her here today was my one big hope. What can I do?"

"I'm very sorry. There are many different types of dementia. It could be related to Parkinson's or Huntington's disease, or if she gets agitated at dusk, it could be sundowner's syndrome. Unless your mother sees a specialist there's no way to know for sure."

My brother Mike flew in the following week with the goal of getting Mom admitted somewhere, somehow. She had stopped speaking to me after the calamity in Dr. Harrison's office. I brought the usual groceries into the kitchen we shared, but otherwise I lived upstairs and she lived downstairs.

The silent tension at home was so dense and dispiriting that as soon as Mike was airborne, I fled for Richmond, where Jack was working on a commercial and had a hotel room. By now I had replaced my junky '95 Sidekick with a zippy black 2001 Miata. The Mazda was a decade old but had a new stereo, with state-of-the-art speakers in which I lost myself.

By phone, I plotted with Mike how to get our mother out of the house and into a hospital. Mike would convince her to go for a leisurely drive to the oceanfront. On the way there, he would happen to get a text from Doc Holliday inviting them to come say hello at the hospital he worked at in Virginia Beach. Once there, Doc would tell Perry she looked very ill and needed to check in for an urgent exam; he would not say she needed her head examined but that's what Mike would call for.

Everything went according to plan—until Doc tried to check Perry in. Mom snapped and became so furious, loud, and profane that they had to close her up in a private room. A nurse gave her a sedative but that didn't help much.

"*I will call the police on you bastards! This is a lawsuit and a half!* Did Danny put you up to this?"

After a few exhausting hours, even though she was still seething, Mom agreed to stay overnight. When I got the call from Mike and Doc, I breathed a sigh of relief from the sanctuary of my hotel room ninety minutes to the north.

"With her son admitting her for delirium we can keep Perry for twenty-four hours," explained Doc.

"They'll give Mom tests overnight to diagnose what's making her act like this so they can keep her longer," Mike added, drained but optimistic.

"I'm *sure* they'll find something," I said. "At this point Mom is bedbug batshit crazy—they'd never discharge someone like that, at least not without meds or a treatment plan." I thanked Doc profusely and told Mike which bars near the house had live music.

With Mom in the hospital finally receiving medical attention, I slept peacefully for the first time in weeks. Jack was up and out to work early, but I lounged in the luxurious king-sized bed with my ringer switched off. I awoke sometime after ten, a new person, full of hope. I checked my phone. There was a text from Mike.

"Mom talked her way out of the hospital. When can you be back? We have to bring her home today."

I felt sick to my stomach. I wanted to climb back in bed and pull the fresh-scented comforter over my head. Before dialing Mike, I called Doc Holliday to learn the details.

"Perry was really awful to the nurse who tried to give her the diagnostic," he said. "Not only did she have rude answers for every question on current events and her mental state, she interrogated the nurse, putting him on the defensive and causing a scene. She is not a popular patient."

"I'm not surprised. But isn't that uncharacteristic aggression a sign of some affliction requiring treatment?"

"You and I know that, but legally it's just a sign that she's nasty. We needed to give her a cranial MRI but she refused. She said if we forced her into the machine, she would wiggle her head to keep us from getting clear images. Perry is beyond stubborn and somehow knows the ropes."

Mom had threatened to wiggle her head to keep from getting a brain scan. What was she afraid of?

As Doc spoke, I flashed back to an odd temp job Mom had in 1979. Another bookkeeping gig—at Long Beach Neuropsychiatric Institute. I recalled her grimacing as she told me about the overhead announcements paging orderlies to clean up a "smear"— when deranged patients smeared feces on their walls or windows. What other alarming incidents had she observed? Did she learn you could nullify an MRI by wiggling your head? For a second, I wondered if she might have been a patient there rather than a bookkeeper, but then I recalled meeting a few of her coworkers. I imagine she witnessed enough heartbreaking psych ward scenes to make her avoid ever getting any kind of mental diagnosis— even if she desperately needed treatment.

I drove from Richmond to Virginia Beach in a daze and picked up Mom. She had nothing to say on the drive home. Later that night I brought Mike to the airport for his flight back to

California. We had achieved the goal of getting Mom admitted to a hospital but with nothing much to show for it.

Now what?

"No more Smartwater—it's not working."

Mom's casual announcement of this change to her grocery list was her only acknowledgment that something was wrong in her noggin. For a moment, Jack and I thought this meant she had regained her sense of humor. Perry hadn't meant it as a joke. Nor was she trying to be funny when she explained to Jack the medical emergency that had caused her to be admitted.

"Did Danny tell you how I lost nine pounds of fluids in two days? It was from an exploding hemorrhoid."

After her overnighter in the hospital, Mom did settle down a little—mainly, I think, because she feared ever having to go through such an ordeal again. She struggled to be more sociable and less negative. To keep our exchanges to a friendly minimum, Mom and I now mostly exchanged notes written in big letters on scrap paper. I scribbled that I was going to the post office, and she wrote, "Need stamps. No flags, no love, no hearts. Elvis, flowers or airplanes ok."

I tried to remain upbeat but I was morose anticipating Mom's next attack. I avoided talking about her mania with most friends and coworkers, as I didn't know what to say without making her out to be a fiend. I was also embarrassed because her delusions had bubbled up since she moved in, but until recently, I hadn't made a big deal about them. Until there was a diagnosis, I would keep mum about Perry's nervous breakdown—or whatever it was.

Out of stupid pride, I also felt like our bleak situation showed that moving Mom in was the colossal blunder friends had cautioned me not to make. Assuming financial responsibility and looking after her physical health was one thing, but how could I deal with her mental collapse when she refused to acknowledge it? At work, colleagues could see I was going through a very difficult period. I could have taken time off, but why would I want to spend days at home? Nights were already more than enough. My saving grace was Jack, who not only helped look after Perry but reassured me that I hadn't made a major mistake.

"This meltdown was precisely why you needed to take her in," he insisted. "Can you imagine her going through all of this on her own?"

After long days at work and tense evenings at home, Jack and I had to build a break into our stressful lives. We needed a distraction from our constant crises, whether related to his impending divorce or Mom's separation from sanity. None of the "48 Suggested Mental Breaks" on Caregiver.com, which included "running through sprinklers," "playing with a puppy," and "making chocolate chip cookies," appealed to us. We found solace in a nightcap at Baron's Pub, the redbrick honky-tonk a few blocks from the house.

We had stopped by the corner tavern for a few tame happy hours before. But hot damn, Baron's boasted a different scene after eleven! That's when one of the brazen all-female drink sling-ers dimmed the lights, a band set up on the grubby carpet, and the late crowd gathered. Among them were brawny shipbuilders from around the world, fey waiters, pensive PTSD patients from the Naval Hospital, and goateed tattoo artists with their well-inked stripper girlfriends. Now an animal activist and a produc-tion designer were among them—not that anyone at Baron's ever asks or cares what you do.

Jack and I were hooked from our first midnight foray. It was a rainy August night. We arrived just in time to watch a blue-grass trio, made up of a father and his two sons, play their last few songs. Their harmonies soared but the way they comman-deered their banjo, mandolin, and guitar warranted a closer look. At exactly the same moment, Jack and I noticed that all three virtuosos were plucking with three-fingered hands.

As the applause died down, Bell Biv DeVoe's "Poison" erupted from the jukebox. A waitress started flinging her mane like an inflatable air dancer in a hurricane. She twerked her rear against each chair of a four-top full of swaying sailors in navy khakis, their afros carved into crew cuts. One reached into the air and made jazz hands to the beat. At the next table, a bespectacled man in a wheelchair was slumped forward. We thought he had passed out. On his way to the bathroom, Jack saw that he was merely texting. With his nose.

On the other side of Jack's empty bar stool sat a young man with a scribbled-up sketchbook and hair like a Three Musketeer. Cascading, well-brushed auburn locks with a mustache and goa-tee. He wore tan, paint-spattered carpenter overalls and no shirt.

His pale, freckled muscular arm reached for the half-finished plate of fries that the stranger next to him had just pushed away.

"Shame to waste 'em," he said with a raspy Deep South drawl before turning to me. "Want some?"

"Sure."

Jack returned from the bathroom, gnawed on a few cold fries himself, and we introduced ourselves to our new friend, JC. Outside the huge white-framed windows, a thunderclap roared and the summer rain cleansed the patio of cigarette butts.

"At least the weather was okay today," said JC.

I thought he was an artistic man of few words, but I was dead wrong. When he got started, he spoke rapid-fire and without punctuation.

"My mom's chicken Henrietta died this morning and she made me bury her out back with her old dead dog and damn it took me a lot of shoveling to find the spot and it's my day off and I hated spending it as a grave digger I'll tell ya."

"That's sweet," I replied, rapt. I hoisted my beer. "To Henrietta."

As we cheered the chicken, a plump blonde flitted by and noticed the cartoons in JC's notebook. "Draw my portrait!" she slurred.

"I don't draw portraits, I do caricatures."

"Whatever—draw me!"

JC rolled his eyes, then looked the girl over and got busy with his pencil. She wasn't unattractive but had a slightly upturned nose and buck teeth. She twirled down the bar, around a few tables, leaned down to chat with the man in the wheelchair, and then returned.

"Well?" she said, excited.

JC swiveled around and displayed the drawing. In it, she looked like Bugs Bunny in a fright wig with the nose of his Looney Tunes sidekick Porky Pig.

"Goddamn you, JC!" she shrieked, flipping him off with a giggle.

JC cackled, grabbed his cigarettes, and went out to light up on the patio, where he huddled with other nicotine addicts under the dripping awning. He ended up becoming a good friend, bringing us to speakeasies, helping with carpentry work at the house, and jibber-jabbering with Mom. She always snapped out of her stupor around him.

Meanwhile, in Los Angeles, my extended family was buzzing about the impending birth of my great niece.

Months before, Perry had made plans to be there for the baby's arrival. After all, it would be her first great-grandchild. I got her a ticket to fly out for it, but unfortunately, when Mom started coming unglued, she had me cancel it. She was depressed about missing the momentous occasion, but sprang to attention with every group text about the baby's predicted arrival. Those updates actually brought us together in the week leading up to the big event.

At last, late one evening, my nephew Andy and his wife, Liz, had a beautiful, healthy baby girl. Her name was Vivien. From the delivery room, Andy sent a joyous announcement with a photo of the newborn to me, Mom, and a dozen other family members.

Mom's phone chirped in her bedroom the same instant mine did in the kitchen. I was washing dishes, but I stopped to take a quick look. In the photo, Vivien was radiant. She had a dynamic smile and—just like her great-grandmother—incredibly expressive blue eyes.

Jack and I were taking a closer look when Mom wandered in clutching her cell phone. I was surprised she wasn't giddy and yelping. Strangely, she was emotionless. Maybe she hadn't read the message yet. Perry slowly put on her glasses and carefully studied the picture of the glowing baby girl she had been so eagerly awaiting. Mom sighed. Looking grief-stricken, she looked at us somberly and made an announcement.

"Dead Vivien. I'll reply and send them all our condolences."

Chapter 19

DOWNPOUR

Violent summer storms sound like soothing symphonies in our little bedroom upstairs. The drumming of a thousand drops a second on the tin roof five feet above, the rattling of the big window in its old pane, the boom of thunder and flashes of lightning bring to mind the cataclysmic "Sorcerer's Apprentice" scene in *Fantasia*. During one such sunrise deluge, I was so mesmerized that I found it impossible to climb out of bed and get ready for work. I also wanted to avoid the torrent of hostility that awaited me somewhere downstairs.

That morning, my go-between—Jack—was back in Richmond. Even though it was the dog days of summer, he was creating wisecracking animated lawn ornaments for a wintry Wal-Mart Christmas commercial. I was home alone with Mom, who was still crossing herself over what she construed as the stillbirth of her healthy great-granddaughter.

To prevent her from bewildering the entire family with hysterical delusions about a dead baby, I had to seize her phone and hide the battery. Because Mom had sent similarly alarming emails about other fantasized deaths, I also cut off her internet. It broke my heart to isolate her like this, but I hoped that feeling of isolation would prompt Perry to want to leave the house, to finally accept help. We stopped speaking for days. Neither of us slept well. We had both become captive in our own home to a menacing lunacy.

I pushed open my heavy bedroom window to let in warm blasts of humid air to counter the chilly air-conditioning. The breeze carried shards of rain and the clean scent of pine trees, which I inhaled deeply, exhaled, and then breathed in again. I was loitering. Finally, I wrapped myself in my plaid bathrobe and begrudgingly began my day.

In my sleep-deprived state, I started down the creaky, dark wooden staircase. I desperately needed to make coffee and turn on some lights. When storm clouds eclipse the sun, our 1870 town house becomes as gloomy as a catacomb, until you switch on the 1970 swag lamps.

Halfway down the stairs, I heard my mother conversing with someone in the living room. Was it the giant cat she had been trying to lure in from the streets? No, this was an engaged discussion, not the baby talk she used with animals. How odd that Perry was even awake at this hour, much less out of the back bedroom in which she had sequestered herself. Had a neighbor come by? Perhaps it was a gas meter reader or someone from the power company fixing a problem caused by the storm. Maybe that's why there were no lights on. I paused and leaned on the banister to listen in.

"And this was the Halloween I went as a flapper, not that you could tell because of the walker, plus kids don't know what a flapper is anyway, but we sure had fun. What did you dress as last year?"

I listened for the response. I could have sworn I heard the faint echo of another voice, but it was drowned out by the rumble of the rain.

"Oh, I bet that outfit was a hit! You should come to our party this fall. Half of Portsmouth shows up. Would you like some more coffee?"

What struck me in my drowsy state was how friendly the exchange seemed. This was a huge relief, as Mom had grown so bitterly antisocial in recent months. As I continued down the stairs to the living room, I was suddenly filled with hope that Perry might be emerging from her mania and was having a pleasant visit with the cable guy.

Peering around the corner into the dim living room, I was taken aback by a scene like something out of Edgar Allan Poe. Old Halloween photographs, illuminated only by an occasional flash of lightning through rain-soaked windows, were strewn everywhere, as if a tornado had rolled through. The only person in the room was Mom, perched on the red sofa in her white nightgown, with piles of photos in her lap, fondly discussing them one by one with an invisible phantom sitting next to her.

Despite the lighthearted banter, Mom's shoulders were hunched, her head tilted unnaturally. The once-wily light in her eyes was switched off. She was now looking at the world through foggy marbles. Her arms gestured randomly, her fingers pointing here or there as if they were on a different schedule than the rest of her. Mom looked like a malfunctioning animatronic ghost in the Haunted Mansion. She was shaking, with splashes of coffee staining her nightgown, as if she could no longer guide a mug to her lips. Her white hair was ratty and twisted. Cold cream was streaked across her face, giving off an eerie sheen in the flickers of lightning.

It was as if Mom were rehearsing a macabre play in a darkened theater, reciting her lines, then pausing for and reacting to the inaudible response.

"And that was the time Danny dressed as Colonel Sanders. He scared the hell out of the trick-or-treaters with the bloody butcher knife. What's that? No, it was made of plastic."

I felt like an absolute idiot for not having instantly recognized this as another invented interaction. By this point, I was so sleep-deprived and desperate that I had become gullible and deluded myself. I stood there petrified and heartbroken. But I knew I had to create a calm façade in hopes of ushering her out of the house and to the nearby hospital in Portsmouth. I figured that was my last hope.

What I desperately had to avoid—at all costs—was putting Mom through the trauma of being carried out of her dream home by force. No men in white coats, no ambulance with flashing lights. There might be a chance she would bounce back from whatever kind of breakdown she was having, but she would never recover from the humiliation of being dragged out in a straitjacket screaming in front of the neighbors. I might never recover from such a scene myself. I had to figure out another route.

The next thunderclap was my cue.

"Hi, Mom," I said with a grin. I stepped over the photos littering the murky living room and sat beside her.

"Good morning, Danny," she replied with a creaky voice. Her quivering lips tried to form a smile and her drained eyes tried to focus in my direction.

"I was just going through some pictures with a friend. . . ." She scanned the room looking for her hallucinatory companion, who had suddenly vanished. Then she swiveled her head back to me.

"What's wrong with me, Danny?"

"I don't know. But let's find out. I'll take off work and bring you right in."

Where would I bring her? The Naval Hospital was around the corner but she wasn't a veteran and they'd never open the security gate for me. Maryview Hospital was ten minutes down High Street. Lots of retirees lived near there. They would certainly know what to do with a broken-down old woman.

"Let's go to Maryview!"

She froze for a moment. Then Mom's troubled face dissolved into an angry grimace, her changing expression lit in silhouette by the daylight seeping through the thin gold drapes behind us. Mom looked like a silent movie star in close-up, going through a range of extreme emotions.

"I am not leaving this house! I don't like doctors and I don't

trust them and I don't trust *you*!" Tears slid down her face in unison with the raindrops streaming down the window.

"I know." I tried to think of a line I hadn't already used in previous attempts to get her out of the house. "Why don't we find a brand-new doctor? There's bound to be one you like at Maryview, and it's so close...."

"*Fuck 'em!*"

She lurched up from the couch. Photos spilled from her lap onto the floor. She shuffled through the dark kitchen to her bedroom and slammed the door. The slamming door always brought me back to scenes from my childhood. That abrupt sound always followed an incident in which Mom fell to pieces for one reason or another. I could not allow another slammed door to be the final word, especially after this latest skirmish. I rushed back upstairs to pull on jeans and a sweatshirt and figure out a fresh approach.

With all the serenity I could muster, I returned to her room and opened the door. Mom was sitting in the dark on the edge of her bed, whimpering, as the percussive rain beat on her window.

"Hey, Mom." She looked up at me, her face devoid of emotion. "You know what?" I continued. "Don't worry about the doctors. You're right—fuck 'em. But you need to get out of the house—let's go to Krispy Kreme!"

That produced a slight nod.

"Maybe," she said vacantly. "But I'm not dressed, I don't know..."

"You've seen the slobs there, don't worry. Just put your coat on over your nightgown and wait in the car. I'll go in and get you a donut and coffee. Doesn't that sound nice on a miserable day like today?"

I pulled Mom's emerald coat from the hook on her door. She stood up and I draped it over her sagging shoulders. With no further discussion, we paced arm in arm through the kitchen, into the hallway, and—praise be—right out the front door.

I walked Perry into the deluge without even stopping to grab an umbrella. The summer downpour didn't even appear to register as she splashed with me through the ankle-deep water to my tiny black Miata. I opened the passenger door, and as she slunk into the seat, her coat slipped off to the drenched sidewalk. I didn't dare take an extra second to retrieve it.

Perry looked like a *Titanic* survivor, a bewildered spinster in a long white nightgown soaked to the bone, as if she'd had to flee the sinking ship in a panic in the middle of the night. We sped off. The Miata skimmed through puddles like a mini-motorboat. The windshield wipers kept Mom spellbound as I raced down High Street toward Maryview. I was afraid to speak, so I switched on the radio and tuned in the big-band station. Billie Holiday sang, *"Summertime, and the livin' is easy . . ."*

The rain was so heavy that Mom was unable to see whether we were really going to the donut shop. That changed when I pulled up to the hospital entrance. Perry suspiciously wiped her foggy window to see big red letters that spelled "Emergency Room" rather than "Krispy Kreme." Her eyes widened with fury as I jumped out of the car and sprinted through the sliding-glass ER doors.

"I need help, please. My mother has gone crazy, I barely got her in the car—she's right outside."

There were only a handful of people waiting in the sterile lobby, along with a tanned, gray-haired security guard.

"Check in at the desk," he said calmly. "I'll go out to help bring her in."

"How old is she?" asked the middle-aged nurse at the admissions desk.

"Does it matter? She's eighty-one."

"I'm not supposed to tell you this but it *does* matter. If we admit her here, they'll just try to keep her overnight, then transport her across the river to Norfolk Sentara. That's the only hospital around with a senior psych ward. Over there, they can decide whether she can be held for care—if they have space. But you have a better shot of getting her in sooner if you bring her there directly. You probably don't want to hear this right now, especially during a stormy rush hour, but if I was you I'd jump back in the car and make a beeline for the Midtown Tunnel. We can't do much for her here."

"Thank you," I murmured, stunned but appreciative.

Another hospital was turning us away. I could not comprehend why hospitals didn't at least have a specialist on call to process psychiatric emergencies like they did for other crises. But now wasn't the time to fret about that. I had a new destination—*the Senior Psych Ward*. Why hadn't any doctors mentioned it before? Maybe it was new. It was so perfectly suited to our case. I instantly thought of it as an impenetrable magical place, like Oz, and would do anything to get Mom admitted, no matter what the gatekeepers said. Maybe we would find a wizard there who would offer a brain to my scarecrow of a mother.

Deep in thought, I rushed back out through Maryview's electronic doors into the rain. Looking up, I saw the security guard sloshing across the parking lot after Perry. She had fled the car and was lurching like a zombie in her sopping nightgown toward the whizzing rush-hour traffic. I now think of that scene as comical, though at the time I was incapable of laughter. I leapt into my car, zipped across the lot, and skidded to a stop on the slick pavement just in time to reach Mom near the curb.

"Let's get the hell out of here!" I jumped out, guided her back into the car, buckled her in, and roared down High Street in the direction we came from. Mom seemed to think we were going home. She sat in the bucket seat dripping wet but expressionless, like her system had auto-shifted into neutral. In hopes of keeping her tranquil, I turned up the big-band station as Lena Horne sang. *"Life is bad, gloom and misery everywhere, stormy weather; I just can get my poor self together, I'm weary all of the time."*

After a few miles, I veered off onto the crowded feeder road that leads to the Midtown Tunnel. Mom snapped out of her trance.

"Where are you taking me?" she pleaded as we looped onto the congested highway. I looked over but couldn't answer for fear she'd try to jump out of the car. Words were useless, so I attempted another form of communication. I gave her a knowing glance, hoping to evoke a remembrance of a lifelong bond of trust and compassion to settle her down. It failed miserably.

I don't know what a banshee sounds like, but I'm sure Mom shrieked liked one. I had never heard her or anyone else make a sound like that. It seemed to come from the depths of her soul and it was terrifying. Then Mom started hitting me, making it even more difficult to steer along the slick, crowded highway. It was the first and only time she ever struck me. It didn't hurt physically; it was just an old lady's fists flailing at my shoulder. Nor did it hurt emotionally; in this moment, I knew she was not herself. She was having a full-on psychotic break—her rage was directed at whoever tried to thwart her, and that happened to be me. I couldn't get upset. Keeping my feelings at bay would keep me steady on the road.

My main concern was that Mom would jump into traffic in the bumper-to-bumper Midtown Tunnel. As Perry wailed and punched, I wormed my arm under her seat belt to keep her in place should she try to flee. She must have read my mind, because now Perry struggled to free herself from the seat belt and grabbed at the door handle—just as we started our descent into the narrow, bustling two-lane tunnel.

The windows fogged up. This made it hard to see, but also prevented oncoming drivers from witnessing what must have looked like a granny fending off a kidnapper. I struggled to keep the steering wheel straight as Mom thrashed like a panicked cat trying to escape. We nearly scraped the tunnel wall a few times as we rolled along in a slow serpentine. My Miata was like a flea buzzing the behemoth Mack trucks heading in the opposite direction to the shipyards. I had to open our windows so that I could see out of the steamed windshield. This allowed tar-smelling road sediment to spatter from the huge truck wheels onto my face and Mom's lap in the low-riding Mazda. We were now wet, manic, and filthy—but we were very close to our destination.

Norfolk Sentara, a sprawling hospital compound, appears immediately after you emerge from the tunnel—*Halleluiah*. I turned into the campus and snaked around toward the ER entrance. Silently I begged the powers that be that I would not again be directed elsewhere.

Outside the crowded, glass-walled emergency room, I pulled up behind an empty police cruiser and lurched to a stop. With one eye on Perry and the other scouring for the admissions desk with the shortest line, I leapt from the car through the automatic doors a sodden mess.

"Which way to the Senior Psych Ward? My mom needs help!"

A thin nurse androgynous as Prince appeared.

"I can help you bypass admissions," he lisped. "Is she Medi-Medi?"

"Yes, thank you!"

As we spoke, I looked outside. Mom was already out of the car. Fortunately, there were no busy streets nearby to worry about. In her wet sooty nightgown, Perry staggered to the police car parked in front of us. She tried to open the back door. It was locked, but she kept at it. Was she trying to hide, or did she think she was under arrest?

"Please tell the orderly to meet me outside," I said.

Out of nowhere, another helper appeared. She was a fifty-something caramel-colored woman with a large build and a calm, compassionate face. Her stained slacks, frayed sweater, and beret told me she wasn't a nurse. I assumed she was some sort of volunteer.

"Don't worry, honey, it's just your mama," she said, grasping my arm. "I'll stay with her outside while you get her registered."

"That would be wonderful, *thank you*." This Good Samaritan stopped me in my tracks with her kindness and managed to draw the only tears I shed the entire morning.

"Wow—you have excellent volunteers here," I said to the nurse, choking back a sob as I filled out a few requisite forms.

"Oh, she's not a volunteer, we admitted her sister last night, she's just a visitor."

Within a few minutes, Mom was in a wheelchair. She wasn't wailing anymore, but remained agitated. We were escorted down a hallway to a bright examination room. The nurse wheeled Mom inside. I hovered at the door and candidly explained Perry's backstory to the busy young physician, whose golden hair was held in a clip. She logged on to a computer and checked the system for notes about Mom's recent discharge in Virginia Beach. She said their senior psych specialists would have a closer look.

"We'll take it from here. Call this afternoon for an update. In the meantime go home and get some rest," she advised with a smile. "Do you need something to help calm you down? I'd be happy to write . . ."

"No, thanks, I want to get through this with all of my wits about me, but I appreciate the offer."

I stopped in a restroom on the way out and glanced in the mirror. Looking back at me with bulging bloodshot eyes was a quaking, waterlogged, mud-spattered beanpole. My chest was heaving. The emotional umbilical cord that had bonded me so tightly to my quirky mother for more than four decades had been shredded. Would it ever heal? Having finally tricked her out of the house and into a hospital with a psych ward, I was filled with relief, remorse, dread, humiliation, and pride all at once. My friends' warnings about the folly of taking Mom in seemed to echo off the sanitized tile walls. Now I couldn't pee. I had to get out of there.

Thankfully, there wasn't much traffic driving back through the tunnel. I switched the radio off and drove in a dazed silence. I was home before nine, when most people were just starting their workdays. This gave me a strange, early bird's sense of achievement. I was too traumatized to cry and didn't want to speak to anyone. I couldn't imagine yammering about what had just happened.

With a blank stare, I peeled off my damp clothes and crawled back into bed. I relaxed by focusing on the hypnotic sound of the calming rain. The droplets were now thumping in dwindling waves. The deluge was starting to let up.

Chapter 20

THE WARD

The Senior Psych Ward was tucked away on the seventh floor of the hospital tower.

Because of Mom's agitated state, the team of doctors agreed to keep her and try to make a diagnosis. I was told to stay away for a few days to give her a chance to settle down and allow them to process the paperwork to keep her against her will for observation. This gave me a chance to collect myself, speak to my brothers, and feel reassured, deep in my weary heart, that I was acting in her best interests.

I walked through a maze of hallways looking for the right elevator bank. After several wrong turns and directions from scrub-clad interns, I found it. I was nervous during the ride up, hoping that my gray slacks and navy button-down made me look credible enough to commit someone. Mom needed serious help, which could be offered only if she stayed long enough for doctors to learn what was wrong.

The elevator opened to a barren, sealed-in lobby. At the far end was a locked door, a red buzzer, and a warning sign that read "HIGH ELOPEMENT RISK." The only time I had ever heard the term *elope* was to describe a joyous young couple fleeing their families to get married. The Senior Psych Ward's occupants were neither joyous nor young, and many were abandoned by their spouses and families. But it's always nice to learn a new use for a word.

I pressed the buzzer, full of dread and curiosity. It was hard to fathom that I had put my mother in a psych ward. Perry had spent most of her eighty-one years evading concern over her "emotional issues"—even cutting off close friends who dared suggest that she see a shrink when she had her meltdowns. This made her a loner for life. Mom probably moved in with me because she knew I wasn't as freaked out as others by her erratic behavior—or maybe she sensed that I was enough like her that it wouldn't matter.

The ward was nearly soundproofed, but as I waited outside the secured door, I faintly heard a patient shouting and ranting somewhere inside. It made me think of the asylum films I quickly flicked past on TCM when channel surfing. *The Snake Pit*, *The Cracker Factory*, and of course *One Flew Over the Cuckoo's Nest*. How could I have my own mother locked up among raving lunatics?

The door buzzed open and I instantly recognized the crazed voice as Mom's. Then I felt sorry for the other patients and almost laughed.

"I'm Perry Lawrence's son," I told the nurse. "I'm here for her commitment hearing."

A commitment hearing sounds like a process to determine whether a couple should marry. Alas, in this case it was to determine whether my mentally ill mother could be held against her will. I don't know what I would have done if they simply discharged her again. I had to keep shooing this thought out of my head like a menacing wasp.

"Do they know what she's got?" I asked the nurse as she led me toward Mom's room. "From what I've read it can't be Alzheimer's, as her memory is so sharp—or sundowner's syndrome, because she often goes to pieces in the middle of the day."

"You'll have to speak to a doctor but I think it's too soon to say. If they keep Perry they'll watch her, try a few medications, and see what she responds to. This could take a few weeks. All I can say to make you feel good is that you have great timing—there's usually a waiting list to get in here. We only have twelve beds, but one opened up just as you were admitting your mother downstairs."

I wanted to tap dance down the corridor.

We passed rooms containing the other eleven patients, most in beds, some in wheelchairs, all silent. I wanted to apologize to them for the lady shrieking down the hall, but they didn't seem to notice. There was a catatonic black gent in an ill-fitting dark suit and a fedora, as if he were ready to hit the town. A few doors down I looked in on an intense, bespectacled granny whose rosy cheeks were buried in a Bible that was literally the size of a matchbook. It looked like a gag gift. Farther along, in the room next to Perry's was a patient with a mop of stringy gray-brown hair covering his or her entire face, reminiscent of Cousin Itt from *The Addams Family*. Itt's head was slumped against a radio that was blasting that classic rock hit with the stuttering chorus: "B-b-b-baby, you just ain't seen nuthin' yet."

You could hear the song's chorus down the hall but the vocal coming from Mom's room was louder. As we approached, it became decipherable.

"Get out from under the bed! Stop listening to my thoughts! You're not a doctor—all you've got is a wellness degree from Mumbai. And you—if you want to do something for me, get me the hell out of this shithole. I've got rights! Obama.com.com.com!"

I started to pity whoever was in the room with her, but the nurse told me Mom was alone. I stood outside the door for a moment, worried that she'd *really* fly into a fury when I walked in. Unbelievably, she quieted right down. She gave me the most serene expression I'd seen in months. I got a rush of relief as Mom reached out and tenderly clasped my hand.

"You're Dan Mathews, aren't you?" Mom smiled sweetly. "Weren't you just in a car wreck?"

I smiled, kissed her forehead, and died inside.

Was she slipping away, never more to recognize me? Would we ever again enjoy one of our acerbic conversations? The nurse led me to a harshly lit conference room across the hall. In the background, Perry lurched anew into another earsplitting, manic monologue. A scene from *The Exorcist* came to mind. The one in which the possessed girl turns suddenly shy and coyly teases the priest for a moment, only to erupt in even more creative vulgarities.

Gathered in the windowless hearing room was Dr. Singh, a pretty neurologist with long black hair and an air of confidence; a mustachioed middle-aged lawyer who served as a patient advocate for the state of Virginia; and a no-nonsense woman who introduced herself as the judge. She had a duffel bag, and as we made small talk, she opened it and removed a long black judge's robe, gently wrinkled like her. I hoped she would grab from her bag a white barrister's wig, too, but she didn't. After pulling the robe over her pantsuit, she put a gavel and an audio recorder onto the table. The proceedings were under way.

"This hearing will determine whether Ms. Perry Lawrence will be committed for further mental evaluation," said the judge into her recorder. One by one, she asked us to lean into the microphone as we introduced ourselves. This was so that we could make ourselves heard above Mom's voice bellowing in the background.

"After the standard examination, it is clear to me that Ms. Lawrence is suffering a serious mental crisis requiring treatment," stated the raven-haired doctor in a slight Indian accent. The judge thanked her and repeated the doctor's name into the microphone.

"From what I have seen I concur with the doctor's findings," said the lawyer with a trace of anxiety.

"Have you interviewed the patient?" the judge asked.

"I tried, Your Honor."

"What was her response?"

There was an awkward moment of silence.

"Counsel, what was her response?"

"Your honor, Ms. Lawrence told me to go fuck myself."

"Thank you," she said, again repeating his name into the mic.

Now it was my turn—and it was no laughing matter, despite the lawyer's testimony. Mom's tirade continued to echo from down the hall: *"Riley, you are my savior! Come back with the strippers at midnight to break me out of here but don't tell anyone!"*

Should I tell them that we actually know a Riley who DJs at a strip club?

"Your Honor, my mother has always struggled with some kind of mental issue. But in the past few years, since I moved her in with me, I've watched her slowly spiral out of control."

"She *lives* with you?" blurted the lawyer. "God *bless* you! I've seen cases not half as bad where the family just gives up." I felt both proud and defensive. Was she really that awful?

"Thank you, counsel," interrupted the judge. "Back to Mr. Mathews; is she a danger to herself or to others?"

"She's not physically aggressive, though she did punch me in the car when I brought her in." I silently reflected on recent scenes. One jumped out. "We live in an old wooden house, and she keeps lighting candles all over the place for people she thinks have died—friends, family, even strangers. She trembles and she's deluded and always seems to find a match. I have come home a few times to a serious potential fire hazard, which was partly why I first sought to get her admitted—unsuccessfully. More importantly, she has been living in a near-constant state of torment for the past few months."

"Thank you," said the judge. "Now please state clearly whether you, as her guardian, believe your mother should be committed here against her will for further care."

"Yes, please, Your Honor."

As with the others, the judge leaned in to repeat my name, but this time she also grabbed the gavel and announced the verdict.

"That was Perry Lawrence's son, Dan Mathews. *Committed.*"

I returned to Senior Psych with Jack the following week, with homemade food for Mom. We also brought gifts for the other eleven patients and the nurses: fancy-looking little boxes of dark chocolates from Big Lots with the price tags ripped off and ribbons tied on.

A few senior psychers were pleased to have a random non-medical interaction. They shook our hands or gave us a relaxed hug, an embrace with a stranger who had no agenda. Not Mr. Fedora. He said "no thank you" without blinking or looking at us. We placed Cousin Itt's box in front of the radio and we think we detected a smile under the droopy locks, but that might've been wishful thinking. On the other hand, Granny with the Barbie Bible dropped her mini-scriptures and grabbed our hands, her fleshy arms wobbling and face filled with joy. "*Oh my word, thank you, thank you! You must be from the church!*" We gave her extra and still had plenty left for the nurses.

We gradually made our way to Mom's slate blue room in the far corner. She wasn't hollering like before. I was both relieved and apprehensive—was she now just a doped-up vegetable?

"Perry has calmed down considerably with the latest medication the doctor gave her," a nurse explained.

"*Thank you.* Is there a diagnosis yet?"

"You'll have to speak to a doctor, I'm afraid, and they've finished rounding for the day." I knew I should've brought nicer chocolates to bribe the nurses. Jack led the way into Perry's room.

"Jacky!" Mom said with a strained voice, lifting her head from the pillow to give him a kiss.

"*Danny!*" She beamed, choking up when she saw me.

PHEW. Mom knew who I was.

Jack and I crouched down for a group hug. The three roommates, reunited in a different room, back to our cordial selves.

I hoisted the bag onto her bed. Jack removed a tub filled with her favorite late-night snack: vegan egg salad with extra relish. Whenever Jack made it at home, we'd find traces on the floor in front of Mom's TV the next few mornings, as she lay slumbering. Mom's hand quivered as she guided a Triscuit smeared with the turmeric-flavored tofu to her mouth. I brought her a box of Goldenberg's Peanut Chews, her reading glasses, and the new Joan Rivers book, *I Hate Everyone . . . Starting With Me.*

"Thank you. I could really use a laugh about now."

"We miss you, but you're looking good," Jack said.

"I don't know about that. I can't even think of when I last had my nails done." Her voice was an octave lower and quavered. Was it from the drugs or was she just exhausted from her fanatical filibuster?

"We'll do that the second you get out of here," I said.

Mom looked at me and smiled, but with a hint of sadness.

"We wanted to bring you vodka but they said absolutely no Absolut," Jack added.

"Damn." She grinned at him. "Just get me out of here soon."

I left her to chat with Jack and went back out to the nurses' station.

"You're right, she seems much better. I understand you can't discuss a diagnosis without the doctor, but what's the drug she's responding to?"

"Risperdal."

"Thanks."

I wrote it down and walked back to Mom's room to find a small group gathering in the hallway outside of her door. A doctor was giving a tour of the facility to half a dozen earnest young interns who appeared to hail from every corner of the globe. They looked like the all-doll cast of "It's a Small World" but in white lab coats instead of native dress. Leading the group wasn't Dr. Singh but another senior psych doctor I'd seen on the ward.

"The patient in here had severe delusions, but she's actually responding to a minimal amount of medication," he told the interns. They smiled at Mom like she was an animal in a zoo whose exhibit plaque they had just read. Perry couldn't hear what was being said but she waved civilly. I wondered if the tubes weighing down her wrist prevented her from giving them the finger. Through her forced grin, Mom whispered an indecipherable comment to Jack, which made him chuckle and showed me that her spirit was on the mend.

"Hi, I'm Perry's son Dan," I said to the junior international assembly.

"Good afternoon, I'm one of the doctors on the team here."

"Nice to meet you," I said, shaking his hand. "Can you tell me what's wrong with her? I've called several times and they told me I'd see a doctor today and you seem to be the only one around."

"I'm sorry," he whispered. "It's too sensitive to discuss in front of a group. But please be relieved to know she's improving. Can you come back tomorrow for a formal discussion?" He warmly put his hand on my shoulder and turned back to the students.

"Ms. Lawrence," he told them, "has a good chance of recovery because she lives in a loving home and has that to look forward to. Unlike most of the others, who don't have much to look forward to at all." The interns smiled and I nodded graciously. I almost got teary-eyed but I was frustrated that they seemed to know more about Mom's condition than I did.

"May I speak with you briefly?" I nagged the doctor. "I understand you are busy but I really need to know what the hell is going on."

He joined me in a huddle a few feet from the group.

"This is hard to explain in a few seconds. Basically, your mother has a brain disorder caused by too much dopamine in her system. It's naturally produced, but some people produce too much. Dopamine is a neurotransmitter—it carries messages from one part of the brain to another so that we function properly. It's rare, but some people produce too much dopamine, which causes them to get mixed signals and act strangely. You follow?"

"Well . . . kind of."

"The drug your mother is responding to . . ."

"Risperdal."

"Yes. That drug absorbs excess dopamine so she doesn't have

the intense hallucinations and fits; her brain isn't getting such confusing signals anymore."

"*Great*. But is it one of those knockout drugs that zone people out? Will it keep her from being . . . herself?"

"It's in the same class of antipsychotics known for that, yes, but a few years ago it was refined to be less sedating so that patients would be more agreeable about taking it. If your mother doesn't refuse the Risperdal, and her system can handle it, I think she'll be in good shape and can go home before long. I'm so sorry but I've got to get back to the tour. Let's talk tomorrow. Stay strong."

I had a wee bit more clarity, but why couldn't he just name the disorder in front of the group? He acted as if Mom had an unmentionable STD.

Jack and I drove back through the tunnel. As soon as we got home, I rushed up to my yellow writing nook, opened my laptop, and looked up the mystery drug on Wikipedia: "Risperdal is an antipsychotic drug used to treat schizophrenia."

Stunned, I clicked on the link:

> Schizophrenia is a mental disorder characterized by abnormal social behavior and failure to recognize what is real. Symptoms include confused thinking, auditory hallucinations, and reduced social engagement.
>
> Schizophrenia does not imply a "split personality"— a condition with which it is often confused. Rather, the

term means a "splitting of mental functions." The main-
stay of treatment is antipsychotic medication. In more
serious cases involuntary hospitalization may be neces-
sary. Genetics appear to be an important contributing
factor.

I am not one to hear voices. However, in that moment I heard
the whole universe harmonize in a chorus of *"Duh!"*

Mom's swift response to the antipsychotic pills brought a meta-
morphic relief to me as it did her. The team of neurologists predicted that she could go home within a week—as long as she
agreed to keep taking the meds and participated in a "family
meeting" to acknowledge her diagnosis.

I had been updating my brothers by phone. Mom didn't want
Mike and Pat to see her in the psych ward; she preferred them
to visit after she was released. A nurse arranged for us to do the
family meeting together by phone in one of the ward's offices. I
envisioned a frank, friendly conversation that would tie up all the
loose ends of this lifelong malaise that had affected all of us.

Sadly, once again, Mom left my brothers, a doctor, and me in
a lurch.

She was already refusing the meds. She denied her diagnosis. She wouldn't take part in the call. Shockingly—despite these
game-changing setbacks—a junior doctor told me he had already
initiated her release.

"We need Perry's bed for another patient."

I immediately wrote to Mom's neurologist and copied every doctor on the ward.

Dear Dr. Singh,

My brothers and I are alarmed about the casual discussion today that our mother, Perry Lawrence, can even be considered for discharge later this week, given that her paranoid schizophrenic state returned with such fury after just two days of refusing her meds. She wouldn't participate in our family meeting today because, in her mind, my brother Mike (who visited last month) "is dead and buried in Hillside cemetery" and my brother Patrick "is busy dealing with his wife's leukemia," despite both of them being on the phone, no death, no leukemia.

Her hallucinations and resulting panic are now so vivid that when I tried to say goodbye today she insisted that it would be goodbye forever because she's convinced she'll be executed in the next room, "where they cut people up, at 9 p.m. tonight." As you saw just before she asked for privacy, she refuses to acknowledge she's in a medical hospital being seen by medical doctors, and won't acknowledge any mental illness whatsoever. She proclaimed that staff members hide under her bed and monitor her thoughts. She is a highly resilient, combative, intelligent individual, and until or unless she is able to acknowledge this and accept treatment, I cannot bring her home, as it is a recipe for disaster. She is even more of a danger to herself and others now than when I brought her in ten days ago, as the rage has grown.

Although she has had signs of schizophrenia as far back as my brothers and I can recall, she only became volatile like this a few months ago, and this state has veered out of control so steadily and rapidly that I fear what's coming next. She has become a different person, one that I can barely recognize. Her behavior today is a huge warning sign of what's in store if she refuses treatment, and it's more than I can handle or be responsible for.

I am eager to participate in her recovery and sincerely hope she can return home soon, but a rush release would be bad news for everybody, especially her. Her sense of persecution and paranoia has become so overblown that I wouldn't be surprised if, in addition to compulsively (and dangerously) lighting candles to mourn the imaginary dead, she resorts to using knives or other objects to defend herself from the "ghosts" who rattle the roof or the actual people who are trying to help her.

This is a heartbreaking letter to write. My brothers and I look forward to discussing realistic options later this week. We hope that the court will approve obligatory anti-psych injections since she won't swallow the pills. If they have the effect of returning her to a comparatively lucid state, we can try again to discuss her condition with her and persuade her to accept long-term treatment. Until then I cannot accept responsibility.

Thank you,
Dan Mathews

Chapter 21

MOM GENES

My favorite place to meditate and read is in the bath.

At six feet five, I cannot fully submerge into our scuffed-up, medium-sized claw-foot tub, but I can lounge for an hour and peruse the latest *New Yorker*, *Entertainment Weekly*, or *Girls & Corpses*. This last color monthly features glossy pictures of babes in bikinis in clichéd cheesecake poses with prop cadavers and skeletons. Whenever the latest issue of "the world's first comedy magazine about death" arrived, I would run upstairs with it like a motor-impaired ostrich and start running the water.

With Perry in an extended stay in the psych ward, I shelved all leisure reading to devour every book I could find on schizophrenia. It was a soggy September as I bathed for hours at a time digesting case studies and considering whether this symptom or that trait gave me insight into my mother's affliction. I must have dribbled a gallon of eucalyptus oil into the bath, as night after night I soaked up stories about paranoia and hallucinations and unraveled families. Only 1 percent of the population is schizophrenic, but because it affects everybody around them, the ripple effect is enormous.

As a history major, I was fascinated to read that schizophrenia is thought by some to be an evolutionary glitch that appeared before the wheel, when humans started developing language. The brain had trouble routing these new complicated audio signals, whereas before it only had to process grunts. We've all dated people who still communicate like that.

I lit a few candles and sank further into my water world.

I learned that schizophrenia surged when the Industrial Revolution drew hordes of simple villagers to bustling metropolises. The chaotic cities clattered with strange new sounds from machines, trains, and even people, who spoke dialects and languages many had never heard. It was a lot for the brain to compute. Health officials soon documented the disorder in every culture around the world, and declared it a distinct mental illness in 1887.

Only in 2011 did scientists trace the gene that causes schizophrenia to the country with the most per capita cases: Ireland. This intrigued me because the only thing my disturbed mother knew about her disturbed mother was that she was the daughter of Irish immigrants. During our Irish road trip when Mom turned seventy, she kept guessing which charming city might hold her roots. She was jubilant when she stepped onto a rolling green meadow so that I could snap her photo next to a "Lepre-chaun Crossing" sign. "We're in the land where fairies dwell!" she trilled in a mock Gaelic accent. Perry didn't know the name of her ancestral town—just that it was "in a western county." Over a decade later, sloshing in the bath in the wee hours, I was riveted to discover in a book called *Stalking Irish Madness* that schizo-phrenia's epicenter is County Roscommon—in western Ireland.

The next night at tub time, I read the book elegant Dr. Singh recommended, *Surviving Schizophrenia*, written to help loved ones cope. It was as dry as I was wet. Still, the section that analyzed the wide range of symptoms held my attention. There are so many variations of the malady that there really is not one clear disease.

I was astonished to read that one sign is the neurological mis-cue to laugh when others cry. Perry didn't have that at all, but I sure did—as evidenced by the soggy *Girls & Corpses* magazine by the tub. I thought back to when I was a child at my uncle Al's funeral. I was shushed in the synagogue for my disruptive gig-gling. It wasn't that I didn't empathize with those grieving, it was just a natural reflex for me to titter at the tears. I never grew out of it, though I learned to control myself. Nowadays I try to get it all out under cover of darkness in a corner at the movies. When a weepy scene has the audience wiping their eyes, I often snicker in my seat. I warn friends of this whenever they invite me to see a tearjerker. A few of them actually ask me along *because* of it.

The next symptom of schizophrenia that made me uneasy was "being in your own world, alone in your head and lost in thought, even among others, noticing things nobody else does." That describes me several times a week. It doesn't take much to lure my attention. I listen for note patterns in the whistles of songbirds while chatting in a park with friends. I analyze the body language of an awkward couple dining on the other side of a restaurant. I imagine what a bedraggled homeless woman outside Starbucks would look like all gussied up. These distractions seldom cause me to lose the thread of conversation, but whoever I'm with can see in my eyes that something else is going on. The question is the same every time: "Is everything okay?" I'm perfectly fine. I'm just enjoying watching the world go by.

My reading glasses fogged as I scrunched down in the warm water reading about these eerily familiar symptoms. I thought again about the genetic link. I inherited my mother's blue eyes, compassion, and sense of humor. Did I also get less desirable Mom genes? Dare I cop to this or that evidence of potential schizophrenic traits? I felt like I should be alarmed. In reality, I was intrigued. My blasé attitude, I figured, is because when I was a youngster Mom taught me to accept another stigmatized genetic condition: I was gay. "You can't change your biology, so you best carry on and leave the shame to someone who actually did something wrong," she advised.

I lay in the candlelit bath and actually felt special. I'm not into fiction, but in the 1990s I read Anne Rice's *Witching Hour*, which follows the magical Mayfair dynasty. In this story, only one child with supernatural powers is born to each generation, and that child is given the mystical Mayfair emerald to symbolize their unique gift. The only jewelry my mother had ever given me as a kid was a mood ring in the 1970s—could that be it?

Finally, I flipped back to reread the prime signs of schizophrenia: difficulty keeping friends and a job, and hearing voices. I have had the same job since 1985 and have more friends than an acid dealer at Burning Man. The only voice I ever hear is my inner voice, which, at that moment, was telling me to add hot water or get the hell out of the tub. I looked at the clock on the sink. It was way past the witching hour. Never in my life have I given much thought to family matters but on this night, there were so many to consider I knew I couldn't sleep yet.

I was most fascinated by the link between schizophrenia and creativity. Many unfortunate individuals hear random sounds in their heads and walk the streets in a spellbound daze. Others similarly afflicted are able to organize the cacophony into songs and become rich and famous. There is also a frequent bond between schizophrenics and creative family members. The bizarre rants of James Joyce's afflicted daughter Lucia left most observers puzzled, but made total sense to her avant-garde author father. Did Perry and I have a similar rapport?

Schizophrenia takes hold when affected carriers of the gene are in their late teens or early twenties, after their hormones have settled. Might any of my young nieces or nephews have it? I took a deep breath of the eucalyptus-scented water and started plotting how to talk with them candidly without freaking them out.

Then I was jolted by a new genetic thought. I had kids of my own—the result of weekly visits to the sperm bank for spending money in college. Because I was tall, blond, and blue-eyed, and because my samples "froze and thawed well," according to the Washington Fertility Center, I sired up to sixty kids. I want to believe they are all fine, but who knows? The disorder can skip a generation. Would I ever be able to talk about this ill-fitting gene with my biological offspring? Were any of them talking to themselves?

I turned on the hot tap for a minute and thought of a quip my drag queen friend Lady Bunny uses: *I went to the psychiatrist, and he asked me if I ever heard voices—I said, YES, Doctor!—and one of them just asked me if I ever heard voices!* I laughed out loud.

"Is everything okay?" Jack called from the bedroom.

"Yeah, I'm fine. I'll be out soon."

Jack knew that was a lie. He went down to the kitchen and poured me a shot of vodka with a splash of pickle juice. The candles made his fit silhouette flicker against the turquoise wall when I gladly accepted the mini-cocktail with my pruned fingers.

"Learning anything interesting? You look like a drowned bookworm."

"Yes, though every answer raises more questions."

For my final week of Book, Bath & Beyond I dove into schizophrenia memoirs. Schizophrenics themselves have written a few. *The Center Cannot Hold* vividly illustrates the anguish of living in a hallucinogenic world. Traumatized family members have written others. *The Memory Palace* is about sisters who moved and changed their names to elude their maniacal mother. It made me think of how I fled the country after high school with little cash and no credit cards. *Henry's Demons* is a diary-style book by a father whose son's psychosis upended the whole family's life. This made me consider my own dad's torment over how to disentangle himself from Mom's manic web while not being an absentee father. He handled the abysmal situation with grace, and I looked forward to refreshing our relationship when things settled down with Mom.

These and other painful printed sagas were fascinating. But the bleak conclusions made me feel like stretching my foot out of the tub and nudging my plugged-in Hello Kitty CD boom box off the counter and into the water.

Last in my damp stack was a brand-new book, *Schizophrenia: A Brother Finds Answers in Biological Science*. It was by Ronald Chase, an acclaimed neurologist. He wrote:

> Because there are virtually no untreated patients with schizophrenia to be found in modern psychiatric investigations, the data on outcomes pertain only to patients taking anti-psychotic drugs and receiving supportive care. The natural course of the untreated disease is unknown, or at least is not described in the professional literature.

I froze in the hot water and almost dropped the book as I envisioned this one.

Mom made it into her eighties without any treatment whatsoever. Her life was littered with schizophrenic tragedies. But she hadn't succumbed to drugs or booze or violence. She may have been a voice-hearing, breakdown-prone, penniless loner of a single mother, but she raised three successful sons and somehow kept her smarts and sense of humor. In Mom's generation, admitting mental illness often meant that you ended up electro-shocked or lobotomized in a terrifying asylum. She used her iron will, sharp intellect, and quick wit to masquerade her affliction almost to the end.

I started to think of Mom as a weary survivor rather than a tragic victim.

I reevaluated a few key aspects of her life. Was Perry in fact hard of hearing like her idol Beethoven? Or did she somehow self-impose deafness as a way to block out all the sounds? Mom's deafness did seem selective on occasion, and she had scored surprisingly well on her latest hearing test.

Mom may have had trouble maintaining relationships with humans—but she enjoyed a deep rapport with other animals. As a result, I grew up highly sensitized to animals. I became a vegetarian activist as a teen and started my career at PETA right after college. Was my life's work inadvertently inspired by my mother's mania?

It was refreshing to find an uplifting trait amid the depressing ones. With that, I emerged from the tub. My bruised spirit had been cleansed along with my lanky body. I felt enlightened, emboldened, and ready to help Mom face her final season.

FALL 2012

Chapter 22

FRANKENSTORM

Mom as Amy Winehouse, with Rose, on Halloween.

Monday, October 29, 2012. As Hurricane Sandy swamped the Eastern Seaboard, I was in upstate New York for a face-off with Cornell University's Speech and Debate Society.

On the elliptical at the Cornell gym, I watched CNN. Lower Manhattan was underwater. Mayor Bloomberg closed the harbor, subways, and stock market. Amtrak halted service from Boston to Atlanta. Airlines canceled flights in all eastern states until further notice. Looking out the window, I could see the ominous northern edge of the storm reaching Ithaca. Would anyone show up for tonight's debate? More important, how would I get back to Portsmouth by Wednesday for our notorious Halloween blowout?

We were now approaching our fifth year in the funhouse.

The place had evolved into a perennial social hub, but our biggest gathering by far was on October 31. On that day, with help from arty friends, Jack, Perry, and I turned our garish Victorian into the epicenter of a Gothic Olde Towne block party. It was like an open house at the Munsters' mansion. There was no way I could miss it. Especially this year. Mom's doctor said it would be a miracle if Perry even made it to the Day of the Dead.

Mom's hardiness had allowed her to forge into her ninth decade as an untreated schizophrenic. But the Grim Reaper was closing in. Dr. Singh explained that Mom's breakdown the previous summer was a symptom of her system shutting down. She no longer had the physical or emotional stamina to keep bluffing her way through the cacophony of voices and noises in her head. That's why she fell apart. Luckily (though I didn't consider it lucky at the time), she had a safe place to fall apart.

Now, with meds—a biweekly shot I made her take at home if she wanted to keep living there—she also had a place to enjoy the tail end of her life. In the end, Mom agreed to the Risperdal injections on the condition that we never discuss her schizophrenia diagnosis. Shortly after she returned home, I emptied the trash basket next to her bed and saw that she had tossed the yellow soda koozie that had graced her Tab cans for eons: "I don't suffer insanity, I enjoy it!"

After her release from Senior Psych, Mom didn't like to go out much. The house became her entire world. Fortunately, we had many friends who loved to enter that world. Especially on Halloween.

"I'm driving back from Cornell right after the debate," I told Jack over the phone.

"I-95 is closed up and down the coast."

"I'll stay on 81, that's a few hundred miles inland. MapQuest says it's 539 miles from here to Portsmouth. The storm isn't too bad here yet. I'll get as far as I can tonight depending on conditions."

"What kind of rental are you in?"

"A Kia Rio."

"Dan! You'll be blown right off the highway. If you're gonna do this swap it for an SUV."

I scrambled to Enterprise, scored a Nissan Armada, and slogged through the outer bands of Sandy to Ives Hall just in time for the debate. I half-expected it to be canceled. Thankfully, about sixty students braved the storm, plus a reporter from the *Cornell Chronicle*, which had already posted an item.

> Should sex be used to promote social change? Watch the Cornell Forensics Society take on PETA Senior Vice President Dan Mathews, who launched PETA's (in?) famous campaign "Rather Go Naked Than Wear Fur" nude on the streets of Tokyo. Following their speeches, Mathews and Cornell's debaters will be grilled by audience members. If you agree with PETA's methods or cannot stand them, don't miss this event!

Cornell was the first Ivy League university to admit women alongside men, so it has long been a hotbed for progressive feminists. New-gen fems came out in force to decry PETA as hucksters of porn. This was five years before campus mania about trigger warnings and safe spaces made the news, so I was taken aback—especially because every student I met there embraced PETA's mission.

By a fluke, I introduced the naked campaign in 1992 at an international fur expo in Tokyo. As PETA's twenty-seven-year-old anti-fur coordinator, I was unable to convince our reserved Japanese sympathizers to target the glitzy fashion show with anything other than a silent Buddhist prayer circle. Out of desperation, my friend Julia and I flew in, stripped outside the expo center, and paraded with a banner proclaiming, "We'd Rather Go Naked Than Wear Fur." We had no inkling the stunt would make global news, launch an ad series, or provoke a PC backlash two decades later.

"In PETA's advertising, women are consistently portrayed as sex objects, with unrealistic and unattainable standards of beauty," began an earnest member of Cornell's team, also named Dan. "Instead of independent agents they are objects for male pleasure. Fatness and unattractiveness is shamed as something that should be avoided by going vegetarian."

At the podium, I explained that as the gay man behind the effort I never saw women as sex objects. Why look at all nudity as porn? Was Lady Godiva wrong to ride bare in her protest? Should we dismiss Michelangelo as a horndog because he sculpted David without clothes? I listed a few notably zaftig or freethinking females who had posed nude for PETA over the years: Carnie Wilson, Melissa Etheridge, Kathy Najimy. The next month, Wendy Williams would unveil her campaign on her self-produced talk show. Like the other models and activists, she volunteered. None had been roofied.

The tit-for-tat went on for more than an hour. It was hard to say which side had the edge. I worried that I sounded defensive or dismissive. When a few speakers portrayed me as a kind of pimp, several students hissed. I wished Mom could see this—that way she would die laughing. At the end, the debate club president took an audience vote. I was stunned when she announced that I won—though only by three votes.

Relieved that the sexual revolution hadn't been a complete failure, I sloshed through the parking lot to my Armada and set sail. Ahead lay two much more tempestuous challenges: Superstorm Sandy and Superfreak Perry. I was determined to make it through the typhoon to help Mom with her very last Halloween getup. People who raise kids are into "firsts." When you assist someone into the grave it's all about the "lasts."

Mom and I shared a visceral, lifelong Halloween bond: she went into labor with me the Saturday night before Halloween, 1964. She and Dad loved to tell me how the obstetrician rushed to the delivery room straight from a costume party. Count Dracula pulled me into this world just past the witching hour. I was a huge baby, so blood splattered everywhere. To this day, I enliven after midnight and remain drawn to costumes, gore, and grand entrances.

As I sped out of Ithaca, the superstitious side of me wondered if I would see Mom leave this mortal coil on All Hallows' Eve to bookend the way she welcomed me to it.

———

I wouldn't have made it past the first Denny's in the Kia. The wind gusts and torrents of rain were unrelenting, but the heavy SUV withstood the weaker effects upstate. I had never seen an emptier freeway. It seemed everyone except for me had the good sense to hunker down. Bored by the time I crossed into Pennsylvania, I pulled off for last call in Scranton. I found a roadhouse jammed with factory workers who had the next day off because of the unfolding disaster. All eyes were on the Weather Channel, which called the Halloween system "Frankenstorm." It looked like the hurricane had washed Atlantic City clean off the map. I called Jack before heading back to the interstate.

"We're both fine," he said. "Your mom thinks the house is going to fly away and land in Munchkin City." They were watching the news and eating tater tots. "Just drive safe and check in later."

When I passed the Virginia state line about 4 a.m., I grew worried. Large swaths of towns had no power. My cell had no service. Sections of the desolate freeway itself were dark. I slowed to a crawl. Small, torn-off branches had littered the road up north. Here giant tree limbs blocked lanes. Barrels rolled across the highway. Where had they come from? I pulled off in Winchester, still 240 miles from home. After meandering around downed power lines, uprooted oaks, and overturned trash bins, I found a motel.

At noon, I checked out and grabbed a copy of the *Winchester*

Star. On the front page was a picture of a pretty blue house very much like ours. Sandy had blown a tree through its roof. I hoped we had fared better. My phone now had service so I called Jack. He said that at dawn, he and Perry were roused from sleep by a giant pine tree crashing down along the entire width of the back deck—just five feet from Mom's bedroom.

"She found it more exciting than scary, and she's been taking pictures all morning. The tree must be thirty feet long and two feet thick. It won't budge." Fortunately, the deck survived. Our long, wrought-iron table took most of the brunt. It had been flattened like a beer can.

Because of the widespread damage throughout Virginia, no tree removal companies could get to us for at least a week. The back deck was where most of the costumed revelers gathered, since the annual affair had outgrown the house. Canceling was pointless as by now people came whether we liked it or not.

"The only person I can think of with a chain saw is that creepy guy with the bloodshot eyes from Baron's Pub," said Jack. "You know—the one who hides in the bushes when he drinks too much?"

"I wonder if he really has a chain saw or just talks about it to freak people out." I pondered our dilemma. "We're desperate. I'll call. I still have his number from when he offered to bring Perry fried rutabagas after she got out of the mental ward."

That evening, I arrived home not to a disaster zone but a regimented sawmill. Luckily I had reached our bar buddy with the chain saw before happy hour. I never knew his profession, but he looked like a lumberjack directing the crew of friends and neighbors. By the time I drove up, he had half the gigantic pine already chopped and stacked. "It'll need to dry but you can use most of this for firewood."

Jack had called out the marines. Well, our merchant marine friend David and a few of his shipmates. They brought smaller saws for the splintering branches. Doc Holliday came to pitch in wearing his fluorescent workout suit, along with John, Roderick, and other Halloween habitués who were not about to let Frankenstorm ruin our Monster Ball.

Mom watched the busy beavers from the doorway leading from the deck to her bedroom. In her white housecoat, she oohed and ahhed and stood by with a pitcher of iced tea. If Sandy had blown the towering pine just a few feet in her direction, Mom would have been smushed like the patio furniture. I gave her a big hug. She would indeed live to see another Halloween—barely.

"At least we didn't lose power," she said. "I read about the tough crowd at Cornell, but I'm proud that you prevailed."

With all that had transpired since last night's debate, I had almost forgotten about it.

That year's Halloween bash drew the liveliest mob yet, probably because people had cabin fever from riding out the three-day storm. There was so much coming and going that the front door remained wide open, oozing fake fog and blasting off-key sonatas from the player piano Jack set up in the foyer.

Inspired by our rip-roaring tree removal, our young neighbor

Ross dressed as Leatherface from *Texas Chainsaw Massacre*. He chased wave after wave of screaming trick-or-treaters with a deafening (de-bladed) version of the power tool. Our tipsy Pentecostal neighbor, Joey, came without a costume, so Mom put him in a dress of hers and had me make him up in old-lady drag.

Rose, a thirteen-year-old PETA volunteer, was the spitting image of chic Holly Golightly from *Breakfast at Tiffany's*. She was Perry's helper and sidekick for the night. They made quite a duo, as Mom dressed as Amy Winehouse, complete with black beehive and white coke residue on her nostrils. Jack's daughter Tess brought her 35mm camera and captured a priceless photo of them on the deck. I wielded an accordion and brought to life Mom's worst nightmare: Lawrence Welk.

Chapter 23

GIVING THANKS

The voices, rage, and paranoia were not all that vanished after Mom grew accustomed to her meds. Over time, she also lost her disdain for leafy greens. With Thanksgiving approaching she eagerly took part in the late-night cooking and tasting sessions Jack and I undertook with whatever weird veggies we found at the international food mart. Even sautéed leeks with Chinese cabbage and cashews, and baked rainbow chard with sesame oil.

Previously, Mom would holler from her bed when she saw one of us scarfing from the pan or eating over the sink. "Don't you people believe in plates and napkins?" Now she giddily joined in to sample concoctions straight off the stove and helped fine-tune the seasonings. She even had Jack snap a photo of her eating rogue-style over the trash can to text to my brothers to get them excited about the upcoming feast. This was a welcome sign that her hallucinations about one or the other dying had ceased.

Another pleasant change was that Mom stopped cranking the TV so loudly you could hear it down the block. She remained very hard of hearing, but she no longer needed booming sound to distract from the voices. Now, when she watched *Bad Santa (Director's Cut)* for the thousandth time, she was content to follow the subtitles.

The effects of the biweekly antipsychotic injection did fade a few days before the next shot, and Mom would grow tetchy. She often complained that she didn't need the next shot and urged me to cancel the nurse's visit. This terrified me. At the nurse's direction, to settle Mom down before needle day, I covertly slipped a quickly dissolving Risperdal tablet into the Vanilla Almond Bark Tofutti ice cream she salivated over at midnight, and life was good again.

The weekend before our guests arrived, we hit Greenbrier Mall so Mom could get her nails done at the Vietnamese salon. She used to have me drop her off near the mall entrance and refused to let me accompany her inside, like a teen embarrassed by her parents. She wanted to stroll in proudly independent. Now she was relieved to have both Jack and me walk her right into the salon. She insisted we get our nails done, too. Jack and I are not mani-pedi queens, but there was no fighting it. We sat awkwardly on the top tier of salon chairs with our jeans rolled up, while Mom turned around from her seat below, giggling and taking pictures until Ngoc told her to sit still and keep her feet in the bucket.

Mom didn't have the energy to get her hair done afterward, so Jack's daughter Mia, who was in beauty school, came over to cut and style Perry's white bob in the kitchen. Jack and I were sufficiently impressed to have Mia hack away at our graying locks, too.

The day before Thanksgiving saw our first arrival. Barbara was Mom's oldest friend, though neither of us had seen her in several years. Like Perry, Barbara was now in her eighties. She flew in on a red-eye but strode up the steps as if she'd just been on a power walk. Jetting around was old hat for Barbara: she was a Pan Am air hostess in the 1960s and even worked one of the first flights hijacked to Cuba.

Barbara had the confidence and style of Diane Keaton. Her great patience no doubt gave her the tenacity to stick by Perry over the decades, despite Mom's bouts of paranoia, which had caused other friends to let go. I always looked up to Barbara—in part because I really knew her only when I was a small child. Now, with our height ratios reversed, I was surprised to have to lean down when we hugged in the doorway.

"Look at you!" she exclaimed, radiant as always.

Mom was fully dressed in anticipation, but lay snoozing on top of her made bed. She dozed a lot nowadays. Both eyes jolted wide open when her old friend sat next to her. I left them to reminisce about the Spanish class they met in during the 1960s and how they saw *Cabaret* opening night at Fashion Island Cinema in 1972. Listening to the animated chitchat, I grinned ear to ear as I brought Barbara's suitcase up the back stairs to the red guest room.

My brothers arrived late that night and stayed in a hotel a few blocks away, across from Baron's Pub. We met there to catch up and discuss Mom's psychological status, which remained a taboo topic in front of her.

"Still no voices?" Pat asked.

"I think they are more like faint echoes now, but only when the drugs start to wear off. Her problems now are physical."

"If only we could have gotten her treated decades ago," said Mike.

"The meds she's on were only tweaked to be less zombie-fying about five years ago. I doubt she would ever have agreed to take them before."

"I'm sure she wouldn't have," said Pat. "But here we are and what a relief."

On Thanksgiving, Barbara and Mom watched the Macy's Thanksgiving Day Parade in the living room by the fire while we boys got busy in the kitchen. Using mock chicken, Pat cooked Fesenjan, a Persian dish with pomegranate walnut sauce his wife, Bita, had taught him. I would eat it every day if I had the ability to follow a recipe. Mike made Mom's trademark Tater Tot Casserole with green beans and celery stock. Jack mashed purple potatoes with rosemary and drizzled Brussels sprouts with balsamic glaze. In the candlelit dining room, I set up the long wooden table with our best mix-and-match plates from Goodwill and a white poinsettia centerpiece.

"*Sooey!*" Pat hollered into the living room. Barbara rose from the couch, but arthritic Perry needed help standing. Jack and I went over to hoist her up, as was now the custom.

"I have to go to the loo," she whispered. We escorted Mom to the bathroom door, but she hesitated before carrying on inside and using the towel racks for balance as she usually did. Rather, she kept a grip on our arms and looked at us with dread.

"Danny, the moment has arrived that we dared not think about. I don't have the strength or coordination to sit and stand. Will you guys walk me over and wait? I don't want Barbara or your brothers to see this."

"Well, I've never minded litter box duty," I said. "Jack?"

"I raised four kids, this doesn't freak me out."

We helped her sit down and awkwardly stood beside her.

"Don't stand next to me!" she huffed. "Go wait by the sink. And for fuck's sake turn your backs!"

We shambled over to the sink as we were told. I whispered to Jack, "If she needs help cleaning herself let's just drag her out back and hose her off." We giggled and Mom shushed us. That caused us to laugh even harder, which in turn caused her to burst out chuckling. I wonder what Barbara and my brothers thought we were doing in there.

"Bon appétit!" said Jack with a slight grimace as he poured a ladle full of mushroom gravy over the stuffing before passing it around.

Gleeful to have made it to Thanksgiving, Mom looked like the Crypt Keeper on ecstasy. She was at the opposite end of the table from Barbara and me and Jack, sitting between my brothers, who took turns telling stories in her semi-good ear. It was hard to tell if she was following, but in any case, she was in heaven.

After dinner, we returned to the living room to enjoy the fire and watch TV. Not another parade and definitely not sports. We tuned in to the History Channel. Earlier that year, Jack had been the set decorator on *The Men Who Built America*, the network's Emmy-winning series about Industrial Revolution titans like Ford, Rockefeller, and Carnegie. Mom had helped him research what their turn-of-the-century mansions and offices looked like. The night before Jack left for West Virginia, where it was filmed, Perry came into the kitchen to see him. She was holding her treasured, antique black-and-white framed portrait of Ellen—the benevolent foster mother who became her godmother.

"She was the one person who loved me unconditionally when I was a child. This picture was taken about 1910, long before I came into her life. I think it would look very nice on Andrew Carnegie's desk in your show. Ellen always admired him for building those beautiful libraries, and she encouraged my lifelong love of books. If there's any way to put it on his desk, it'd be a tremendous tribute and I'd die a happy old lady."

"What a cool photo, of course I'll do it. You never know what the director or editor will chop out so I can't promise anything, but I'll place it where I think it has the best chance at screen time."

The show had debuted Thanksgiving week, and we recorded it to watch the Carnegie episode together by the fire. My brothers, Barbara, Jack, and I made ourselves comfortable on the couch and red velvet thrones, but Mom stood leaning against the armoire with the TV so that she could watch up close.

We clapped when Jack's name whizzed by in the opening credits, but grew anxious as we skipped past the commercials to the scene in Carnegie's office. The screen faded up from black and Campbell Scott's narration began. The camera slowly panned to reveal Carnegie's elegant study. When his ornate desk entered the frame, the camera held firm for several seconds. The static shot revealed—clear as could be—the framed photo of Mom's god-mother, Ellen, as if she were a Carnegie herself.

We all jumped from our seats and cheered, like we were watching football with the rest of America and our team had scored a touchdown. Mom softly gasped and touched the screen.

"She's in eternity now," Perry said calmly, her eyes moist. "Thank you, Jacky." He rose and hugged her tightly. As their embrace lingered, Mom looked around at the rest of us and said, "It's an orphan thing." With that, Mom shuffled off to bed.

Chapter 24

HAPPY DEATH DAY

"Life does not cease to be funny when people die any more than it ceases to be serious when people laugh."
—George Bernard Shaw

Mom in a mask somebody left on Halloween.

December was nigh. Somehow, Mom lurched along, like the mystifying Ghost of Christmas Yet to Come. But the ol' girl kept her spirits up.

Jack's ex, Anna, had an early holiday party at her house in Norfolk, with all four kids. Their eldest son, Dylan, had a brand-new baby boy, Micah. Eager to meet the new addition, Mom agreed to come along for a short while. This astonished us, given her weak condition.

Anna, knowing well how deaf Perry was, surprised her with a gag gift: earphones with an attached mic to hold up to whoever was speaking. The contraption fascinated Mom, who instantly put on the headset. However, instead of pointing the mic at someone else, she started singing. To herself.

Swing low, sweet chariot, coming for to carry me home
Band of angels coming for me, coming for to carry me home

She closed her eyes and belted the spiritual as if auditioning for *America's Got Talent*. As the kids laughed and applauded, Mom remarked, "It's been a long time since I've heard that."

Only Jack and I knew that she was somehow reclaiming the death dirge that had haunted her for so many years. We also knew that the "band of angels" coming for her would soon be descending.

After half a glass of wine, we popped into the dim bedroom where Micah was napping so Mom could meet him before Jack and I drove her home. Dylan lifted his baby out of the crib and handed him to me. Micah's eyes—big and friendly just like his dad's and grandpa's—fluttered open to see Perry's gentle face cooing at him. He cracked a cherubic smile. I wiggled his two-month-old hand at my eighty-two-year-old mother, leaned in to his ear, and whispered, "Say hello, and wave goodbye."

Back at home, we walked Mom to her bedroom, but she stopped just shy of the doorway. Out of the blue, she pulled Jack and me in for what we assumed was a good night hug. Then she started trembling.

"What's the matter?" Jack asked.

"Nothing's the matter," she sniffled. "Not anymore. We made it—*we made it*! And now I have to go. But I love my life here with you two so much that I don't want to leave. I'm not afraid of death, I just wish I could keep going for a little while longer now that I'm . . . better."

The three of us huddled weeping and wordless. This was the closest Mom would get to acknowledging the unspeakable mania she had struggled to ignore. At last, Mom was on the other side of the mental hurdle that plagued her life. It was sad that this resolution happened so close to her death, but at least it happened, for which I shall be forever grateful.

After that, Mom barely got out of bed. Friends began coming over every night. Our neighbor Brian, a handsome, noir navy pilot, offered to sit with her so that Jack and I could DJ at the roller derby, an ongoing gig since we met a few of the tough, gorgeous skaters at Baron's. When we got home, we were surprised to find that Brian had decked out Perry's bedroom with twinkling Christmas lights and garland. He sat next to her bed, both of them smiling at his handiwork.

"Brian should have our rosebushes when I'm gone," Mom said softly. "His front yard gets better sun than we do out back." They thrive in Brian's yard today.

When the psych nurse came to give Perry her next shot, he noted that she was much more delirious than on his previous visit before Thanksgiving. I explained that she mostly slept, could no longer manage the bathroom, and her eyes were starting to mist over. He called the agency.

"Miss Lawrence is transitioning to home hospice." A new nurse would be coming, mostly to make sure Perry was comfortable as her chronic lung and heart problems—the ailments that almost kept her from moving to Virginia—started shutting her down.

It might take a week or two, but Mom would die at home. Not in a scary psych ward, an antiseptic senior center, or a bland hospital room, but in our very own home. After all the terrifying episodes we struggled through over the past four years, I was overcome with relief. This was why I had bought the house, after all, not just for her to live in but to die in. It had all been worth it. I felt like a proud parent who had put his kid through college and was anxiously awaiting graduation day.

Some think I'm too blasé about death. It may be that I used up my lifetime allotment of grief in the AIDS era—two decades during which I watched dozens of young friends shrivel up and die. At some point, a coping mechanism kicked in. I was more useful when I suppressed my own feelings and just tried to keep the latest victim in good spirits as death approached. It felt selfish to break down among those who needed strength. Of course, when nobody was looking, I bawled like Tammy Faye Bakker.

That desperate outlook naturally resurfaced when Mom started going down.

Perry's home hospice nurse introduced herself as Fifi. She was soft-spoken with loud hair, bright pink, which stood out starkly on her smooth, dark complexion. When Perry asked her to write her name out, she spelled it "Fee-Fee." The quiet nurse exuded an inner strength that allowed her to keep cool no matter the suffering she witnessed.

"How did you get into hospice care?" I asked as I made her coffee.

"My mother died when I was twelve. I was so devastated and ill-prepared for the situation that I decided to devote my life to making it easier for other people."

Fee-Fee came every weekday to sort Mom's meds, change bedding, heat soup, and help her to the bathroom. Mostly, she read romance novels as ghostly Perry dozed with her mouth ajar. When Jack and I got home from work, Mom sometimes roused for a few minutes, and we all shared in the obligatory hospice banter.

"Have you had any discussions about . . . the inevitable?" Fee-Fee asked plainly.

"Yes," Mom gasped with a teasing smile. "When the time comes, Danny asks that I try to hold on till Thursday." She took another breath. "Because on our street, they haul away the trash on Fridays."

"That's *terrible!*" said Fee-Fee, shaking her head as Jack fluffed Perry's pillow. Grinning, the nurse continued, "These conversations don't usually end on a funny note."

A few days later, Mom's eyes clouded over so much that she could no longer make out the photos in the bird-watching guide she kept on her nightstand. Losing her hearing and her marbles was tough—but losing her sight was intolerable.

"A life without books is no life at all."

That was one of Mom's last sentences. From then on, she exerted her last bit of control over her destiny by refusing all meds except painkillers. Fee-Fee nonchalantly nodded her approval.

With D-Day looming, David, our gardener friend who had helped me test Mom's meds, drove down from DC. He stayed in the guest room directly up the back stairs from where Mom lay. David bunked over to help Jack and me make Perry's last few days as blissful as possible. The three of us perched dutifully around her bed like ladies in waiting.

Mom's breathing slowed down so much that, several times, we thought she had actually passed away in her semiconscious slumber. We held our own breath, only to have the silence broken by her wheezing death rattle, which seemed to sputter out in synch with the blinking lights illuminating the pink-carpeted refuge.

To make Mom's last lucid moments pleasant, we arranged her favorite dolls around her sippy cup on the retractable hospice table. Pee Wee Herman, Dr. Frank-N-Furter, and the rat king from *Nutcracker* stood among busts of Beethoven and Jesus Malverde. When her cloudy eyes flapped open for a few seconds and she made out the display, Mom looked toward us, clasped our hands, tried to stretch her lips into a smile, and dozed off again.

On a windless blue Sunday morning, Mom calmly exhaled for the last time. Only the dolls and I were at her side. David had gone out for coffee and Jack was showering upstairs. I kissed her cold cheek and clung to her bony hand. Though I had tears in my eyes, I felt more stoic than sad. All the pain and confusion, stretching back decades, seemed to evaporate into the ether with her last breath. All I could think about was how magical it was to be her son.

"Thanks, Mom," I muttered as I leaned in for a final embrace.

I was uneasy about how to show my emotions. Was I supposed to cry? Should I replace my red pajamas with a black mourning ensemble? Should I feel guilty that I had kept the receipts for Mom's Christmas gifts?

"Bloody Marys will help us assess our moods," said David. As we awaited the crew from the mortuary, Jack uncorked a bottle of Luksusowa and we drank our breakfast. Starting, of course, with a toast to Perry—and as many of her other names as we could recall.

Now what?

Music was required to ease the harsh silence. Jack fetched the stack of old vinyl holiday records we trot out each season. Truman Capote's lispy *Christmas Memory* was too cerebral. *Christmas with the Crickets*, in which the voices are sped up to sound like insects caroling the classics, was too silly. Then I came upon *The Nutcracker*. It has somber touches but exudes joy. As it was Mom's favorite, I plopped it on the turntable, cranked the volume, and carried our cocktails on a tray to the porch swing to await the body snatchers.

Tchaikovsky's sister died shortly before he composed *The Nutcracker* in Russia in 1892. Some say that inspired the sad, recurring downscale melodies in the otherwise upbeat score. That sure made sense to the three drunks absorbing every note of it on the porch in Portsmouth that bright December morning.

The graceful "Dance of the Sugar Plum Fairy" was playing as the husky women from the funeral home clopped on the hardwood floor pushing the gurney with Mom's body, zipped up in a dark blue bag. Jack followed the procession holding aloft Perry's glamorous 1940s head shot to show what she looked like in her prime. I jumped around snapping pictures like it was a Bat Mitzvah, just as Mom did during any significant happening. David just watched, one hand holding a glass and the other mock-conducting a classical orchestra with a dribbling stalk of celery.

In this moment, the poignant music inspired David to have a brilliant idea.

"You know what," he said. "My ex's production of *Nutcracker* opens on Friday. He only met your mom once but he *loved* her. As a send-off, why don't we ask him to put Perry's ashes in the snow that falls at the end of Act One?"

I was flabbergasted. This choreographer presided over a major East Coast ballet company. The idea of any sort of memorial had not occurred to me yet. With the holidays around the corner, I was loath to throw together a sad, last-minute tribute. What would my brothers in California think?

"Yes!" I screeched. "If we can get her ashes in time."

Mom would have loved this scheme so much that I wanted to call the mortuary and ask them to preheat the oven. The quirky choreographer—who wishes to remain anonymous—hit it off with Perry a few Christmases before, when he placed us in box seats at his renowned *Nutcracker*. David got him on the phone and Jack and I hovered to hear his reaction.

"When I met Perry she made me feel like the most talented person on the planet," he said wistfully. "She was a true aficionada of ballet." After a few seconds' pause, he declared, "I'd be *honored* to choreograph her grand finale."

It all came together like a big gay conspiracy. Each of us— Tchaikovsky, the ballet director, David, Jack, and me—was queer. Mom would have beamed. After decades of disastrous marriages and romances, she would make her farewell as a grand dame among gays.

It felt predestined that Perry would die just before the holidays so that Tchaikovsky's wintertime masterpiece—her beloved *Nutcracker*—could be her exit music. When I was a clumsy twelve-year-old, Mom convinced me to audition for a touring production of *Nutcracker* in California. Somehow I landed the role of a dancing rat. Learning poise and performing my divertissement before a thousand people each night was a big confidence builder during my chubby, closeted adolescence. Perry never missed a show—but I could tell she'd have rather been onstage than in the audience.

Now, I would finally be able to return the favor as Mom—or what was left of her—would glimmer among the corps de ballet in this Christmas spectacle.

Chapter 25

THE POINTE OF NO RETURN

"There was a bit more of the ashes than I expected so I spread Perry out in different areas," the choreographer texted during the overture. "Some of her is in the snow, some of her is stage right, some is stage left, and some is in the center just in front of the Christmas tree. I also put a little in the rosin box so she'll go out in the dancers' pointe shoes throughout the performance."

A rosin box is an urn fastened to the floor just offstage at the ballet. It contains a white powder pulverized from pine sap, into which dancers pat their bare feet to absorb sweat so they don't squirm inside their slippers. After a ballerina ties the ribbons of her satin pointe shoes to her ankles, she dips into the rosin dust once more to prevent the slippers from sliding on the wooden stage she twirls across on the tips of her toes.

One of the regrets Mom had in her thorny life was not pursuing her dream to become a ballerina, to push the confusing real world aside for a stage full of wordless music, grace, and joy. In death, however, the dream came true. The lithe choreographer carried out the funereal task just before the opening strains of the *Nutcracker Suite* prompted the elegant, sellout crowd to take their red velvet seats.

I had just phoned my brothers with an update from the souvenir stand in the lobby, where I bought *Nutcracker* tree ornaments as mementos for them and my nieces and nephews. Mike and Pat agreed this was the perfect tribute, as long as I saved some of Mom's ashes for them. "There's plenty left over," I explained. "We just sieved out the most powdery part. We couldn't have dancers tripping on dental work."

From our seats in the seventh row, Jack, David, and I could see white wisps of Mom puff up from the stage like happy little ghosts as the divas spun into pirouettes in the bright spotlights. I was elated to see Perry's residue involved in such a physically challenging expression of beauty since less than a week before, on her deathbed, she didn't have the strength to speak or swallow, much less walk or dance.

Though mesmerized by their whirling feet and outstretched arms, I was equally drawn to the dancers' proud faces, each of them chin-up. The regal, confident smiles of these artistes displaying such control over their bodies helped restore my own crumbling composure in the wake of caring for my darling, deaf, demented drama queen of a mother.

In our winter finery at the historic theater, we were downright giddy through *Nutcracker*'s cheerful opening party scene. But toward the end of Act One, when the solemn "Journey through the Snow" unfolds, the gravity of the occasion finally enveloped me. That song's pensive, slowly mounting exchange between the string section and the horns brought to mind the tragic journey through life Perry faced as a schizophrenic, her beauty and wit marred by a paranoia that doomed one relationship after another. She was like a flowering cactus, dazzling to behold but piercing to touch.

I sat frozen in my seat as traumatic scenes from Mom's life flickered through my mind: fleeing her psychotic mother for an orphanage, having her first children taken away, living in a Salvation Army, being stalked and raped. The thunderous orchestra provided a stirring sound track for this stumble down memory lane, and I started sobbing in my seat. It was that overwhelming moment of emotional release most people reserve for the lowering of a casket or winning the lottery.

Then, as that beautiful dirge gave way to the more up-tempo "Waltz of the Snowflakes," my mood boomeranged. The magnificent melody, punctuated by the lush harps and flutes, helped purge my grief.

Act One's finale was upon us.

The vigorous dancers in white soared and twirled to the cellos and flutes until the crescendo. Then, the angelic chorus signaled the snow to begin cascading onto the stage. Down it came, in twinkling flurries. Among the fake flakes was my actual mother, whose fresh, finely sifted cremains floated like confetti in a ticker-tape parade. As the strings and the snow swirled, my tears of grief became tears of joy.

These four tumultuous years left much to contemplate. A standard, spoken memorial would have been impossible for me to conceive. The surge of extreme emotions I felt was much better articulated—and soothed—by this spectacular symphony. I had only started to process it all. There was a lot more to sift through than ashes.

Epilogue

LIFE GOES ON

"People who live in difficult circumstances need to know that happy endings are possible."
—Sonia Sotomayor

I'm glad Mom didn't kill herself when she fled to Vegas in 1954. But I wish she had been there in 2014 to see me and Jack get married.

We were among the first gay couples to legally wed in the Marriage Capital of the World. Our public ceremony under the "Welcome to Fabulous Las Vegas" sign was front-page news in the *Review-Journal*, which quoted our sacred vows: *"We've been waiting for gay marriage to be legal in Vegas so we could have as tacky a wedding as any straights."*

Our marital flash mob even made the *New York Times*, which identified me as "a son of the late Perry Lawrence, who lived in Portsmouth, Va." Since Mom's birth certificate listed no name or residence, I was tickled to see both in print after her death.

We transformed Perry's bedroom into a disco den. Her beloved bust of Beethoven presides over the turntable. We ripped out the cat-shit-flecked carpet and refinished the original 1870 hardwood floors. With help from friends, we painted the top half of the walls parakeet green, lined the lower half with black-and-white-striped wallpaper, and glazed the molding in between Cherry Blossom Pink, in honor of Mom's nails.

Perry's former lair also became a favorite haunt for—dare I say it—the grandkids. Jack and Anna's brood were young adults when I met them but I got to know the four grandsons as soon as they were born. I'm the giant they climb on and jump from in the Virginia Beach surf. My back can hack it because a new procedure came along: stem cells from my hip were injected into my spine to regenerate my defunct discs. I could balance Dylan's five-year-old Micah on one shoulder and Mia's four-year-old Oakley on the other as they played High Dive.

They call Jack Grandpa and me "Danpa."

One Sunday, Jack and I dawdled in the backyard cleaning up after a party. A bar buddy recovering from PTSD at the Naval Hospital was being sent home, so we hosted a farewell dinner that turned into an all-nighter. Lugging bags full of empty beer cans, we sat on Mom's cat bench and reflected on how glad we were to have kept the house. "This place was such a burden," I said. "Now I can't imagine living anywhere else. I hope Perry is just as happy wherever she is."

Suddenly, we heard a rustling in the ivy behind the bench. We turned around to see what looked like the top of a massive, marauding raccoon. The animal took a flying leap and landed on the little stone bench right between us. This was no raccoon. She was a Manx—the huge cat Mom had been trying to lure in from the street during her last year. A neighbor had moved and left her behind.

Previously, this feisty gray stray never got within feet of us. Now she was a purring blimp with paws outstretched in search of affection, splayed so that she clasped both Jack and me at once. Manx are a stocky breed born with stumps for tails. This one looked up at us full of love, chest down but pointing her quivering nub of a tail skyward, like E.T.'s magic finger.

"Remember when Perry said that after she died she would make contact at the cat bench?" Jack laughed. "Maybe this is it."

We meandered down the path to the house to see if the feline would follow. Sure enough, she sashayed right behind us, like Mae West without a girdle. She came inside and never left.

Making tacos, we tried to think of a name. Chopping cilantro, I was inspired.

"Is 'Cilantro' gay enough?"

"It will be if she ever gets out and we run down the street hollering it."

"So be it!" I said, leaning down to kiss Cilantro on the head.

It was nice to have a new lady of the house.

Acknowledgments

For their input and encouragement, I would like to thank Peter Borland, my longtime editor at Atria/Simon & Schuster, Judith Curr, Bill Clegg, Will Lippincott, Tom Eubanks, Ollie Hallowell, Rick Weiss, Karla Waples, Connie Pearson, Gail Gibson, David Cohen, Lee Knight, Ingrid Newkirk, Carol Schaefer, Westley Keith Knight, Joan Mathews, and Johnny Machuzak.